How to Achieve Glowing Health and Vitality

How to Achieve Glowing Health and Vitality

Paramhansa Yogananda

Crystal Clarity Publishers
Nevada City, California

Crystal Clarity Publishers, Nevada City, CA 95959
Copyright © 2011 by Hansa Trust
All rights reserved. Published 2011. Reprinted 2015

Paperback ISBN: 978-1-56589-256-9
ePub ISBN: 978-1-56589-508-9

Printed in China
3 5 7 9 10 8 6 4 2

Created and produced by Crystal Clarity Publishers

Library of Congress Cataloging-in-Publication Data

Yogananda, Paramhansa, 1893-1952.
  How to achieve glowing health and vitality / Paramahansa Yogananda..
    p. cm. — (The Wisdom of Yogananda ; vol. 6)
  Includes index.
  ISBN 978-1-56589-256-9 (pbk.) -- ISBN 978-1-56589-508-9 (ebook)
  1. Health. 2. Vitality. 3. Diet. 4. Exercise. 5. Mind and body. I. Title.
RA776.5.Y58 2012
613--dc23

                          2011041783

www.crystalclarity.com
clarity@crystalclarity.com
800-424-1055

Contents

How to Achieve Glowing Health and Vitality

Chapter *1*

Vitalize the Body with Life Force

Draw on Limitless Cosmic Energy

Right beneath the flesh is a tremendous current.
By the pickaxes of Self-realization,
I have found that Life Force again.
I and my Father are One.
I am not the flesh.
I am a bundle of electricity *behind* this body.

Cosmic Energy is within and around you, recharging the body at all times with vitality. You can call on that eternal supply to make the body fit in every respect. A perfect body, free from disease, presents less resistance to the practices for attaining Self-realization.

Most exercises stimulate only the muscles and thus the animal consciousness, not the subtle nature. Now you will learn how to concentrate on your Life Energy and will power, and to experience your subtle spiritual nature. Life and strength do not depend solely on food or exercise, but are sustained from the powers within. A dead man cannot be brought back to life by filling him with nourishing food, nor can he become strong by artificially making him exercise with dumbbells—because his Life Energy is absent.

Our thoughts, will, feeling, muscular strength, proper action of organs and glands—all depend for their existence on the Life Force. Billions of body cells are kept alive and properly working through this secret vital power.

The human body is surrounded by a halo of conscious Cosmic Energy. Through vibrations of Cosmic Energy, God's intelligence supplies our bodies with Life Force. The medulla oblongata, the "mouth of God," is the antenna that receives energy from Cosmic Consciousness.

By consciously willing, you can draw Life Energy into the body through the medulla oblongata to replenish the energy that is expended through thoughts, feelings, and physical activities. The will bridges the gulf between Life Energy in the body and the Cosmic Energy surrounding it. If you follow these teachings, you will learn to draw on Cosmic Life Energy to vitalize every body cell. You will experience yourself *as Life Energy*—and not merely as a body of bones and muscles.

Exercising with will and concentration draws energy directly into the body. This energy is quickly absorbed by the muscles, blood, bones, and sinews for cellular rejuvenation. The Yogoda exercises give the highest degree of energy with the least tissue destruction.

The greater the will, the greater the flow of Life Energy. Angry men and angry animals manifest abnormal strength. This abnormal strength is not due to their muscles growing stronger during the short period of their anger. Their will, stimulated by anger, causes an extra flow of Life Energy or strength into their bodies.

You should depend more and more on the limitless supply of Cosmic Energy, and less and less on other sources of energy. Eating all the time will make your body get old more quickly. The only way to keep the body rejuvenated is to unite human consciousness and Cosmic Consciousness.

The mind must never be hypnotized by human limitations of sickness, old age, and death, but should constantly, inwardly remember: "I am the Infinite, which has become the body. The body as a manifestation of Spirit is ever youthful."

How to Recharge the Body with Energy

First, lift your arm and then drop it. What lifted your arm? Will power and energy. Now close your eyes. Can you lift your arm without willing to do so? Can will power alone do it? No. It requires both will power and energy. Will power is the switch that controls the flow of energy.

But do you know how will power and energy do this? The answer is: by flowing into the different parts of the body. We want healthy muscles, bones, marrow, blood, and tissues; in each of these the energy is like a battery. Just as an automobile battery needs both electricity and distilled water to keep it alive, so the body battery needs recharging with life force through the medulla, as well as food and other physical means of sustaining life.

Electricity changes distilled water into the force that recharges an automobile battery, and Life Energy converts oxygen, solids, and liquids into the force that keeps us alive. Foods have come from this Life Energy, and when you put them into your stomach they must again be converted into energy to be used by the body. Your supply of energy depends on the chemicals you take into the body and on the energy taken in through the medulla.

Comparison of Mechanical Movement and Will

EXAMPLE 1

1. Extend the right arm in front of you.
2. With the left hand lightly grasp the biceps of the right arm.

3. Bend the right arm at the elbow, and notice the automatic contraction of the biceps through the mechanical movement of the arm.

Note that the action of the will is in the bending of the arm and not in the contraction of the biceps.

EXAMPLE 2

1. Relax the right arm loosely at the side.

2. With the left hand lightly grasp the biceps of the right arm.

3. Close your eyes.

4. Without bending the right arm or making any other mechanical movement of the arm, slowly tense the biceps to the maximum with will power.

5. Relax slowly.

Note that this tensing of the biceps, if done successfully, is the direct action of the will on the muscle. (If you are not successful in tensing the upper arm, try the experiment with the forearm, which may be easier for some people to tense.)

ॐ ॐ ॐ

Energy and Will Power

Lift your right arm parallel to the ground with upturned palm. Hold it there. Note that a certain amount of will and energy holds your arm in this position. If you remove the will power from the uplifted right arm, the arm will fall, drawn by gravity, and will hang by your side. The arm will also fall if the energy is withdrawn.

Now raise your right arm and tense it as much as is required to hold an imaginary weight of five pounds. Then tense it in order to hold an increased imaginary weight of ten pounds. Tense it still further to hold an imaginary weight of fifteen pounds. Now relax and drop your arm.

Whether holding an actual or an imaginary weight of five pounds, you have to *will* to hold it and you have to use an appropriate amount of *energy* necessary to hold it. Similarly, when you will to hold an increased weight of ten or fifteen pounds, you increase your will power and the amount of energy sent to the arm in order to hold the greater weight.

This experiment of lifting imaginary weights proves that an act of pure consciousness, or will, produces actual energy in a body part. Will power is the invisible switch of consciousness that sends energy to any body part and produces tension in that part. It is a physiological fact that the more we apply will to a particular spot of the body, the greater is the flow of the electric nerve current to that spot, and the stronger is the muscular movement caused thereby.

By *imagining* that you are sending energy to the right arm, you may succeed in sending a faint current there, but by *will power* you perceptibly send energy. By *willing* to energize the right arm, you arouse energy felt as power, and you create tension in the muscles.

Will is the prime factor in creating changes in the flow of energy to muscles or to any body parts. You discover the great relationship between will and energy: "The greater the will, the greater the flow of energy."

An Exercise Using Tension

Sit on a chair. Tense the whole body and then relax, keeping the body motionless. Then bend forward with arms down and, clasping your hands together, hold an imaginary cord tied to an imaginary weight of twenty-five pounds. Now send enough will power and energy to lift twenty-five pounds one inch from the ground—tensing the hands, forearms, upper arms, then chest, abdomen, hips, thighs, legs, and feet. Now use more tension and continue lifting the weight higher: two inches, six inches, one foot. It is very heavy.

Then drop your imaginary weight and sit back in your chair, relaxed and motionless.

When you grow stronger, lift imaginary weights of thirty to forty pounds—try to employ the exact amount of tension required to lift an imaginary weight of a certain number of pounds. Then relax. (The best way to know the exact amount of energy required to lift an imaginary weight is to lift the actual weight and feel how much will and energy are required.)

Degrees of Tension and Relaxation

Tension results when energy is sent by will power to any muscle. There are varying degrees of tension, depending on the amount of energy sent to the muscles. We shall consider the three degrees of low, medium, and high tension. Low tension is a small amount of energy; medium is more; and high is as much as possible. The withdrawal of energy from the muscles is called relaxation. This may also be in three stages or degrees, resulting in partial or complete relaxation.

You may be able to distinguish between them by trying the following exercise: Raise your right arm forward, parallel to the ground; grasp your forearm just below the elbow with the fingers of your left hand, and press gently. Now, hold your right forearm still and relaxed with drooping palm and fingers, and feel the degrees of tension:

1. Low tension: Partly close the fingers of your right hand and note the low tension of the muscles in your forearm.

2. Medium tension: Close your fingers half way and feel the medium tension.

3. High tension: Close your fingers tightly and feel the high tension.

Now drop your arm to your side. With closed eyes, tense with will to high tension. Now, open your fingers so that they are half open; then open your hand so that it's almost completely open; then let your fingers relax completely and your hand droop. You thus experience the degrees of relaxation, ending with complete relaxation of those muscles.

During relaxation, pay attention to the gradual withdrawal of energy and loosening of muscles. ("Relax and feel.") With tension, energy can be drawn into the body, and by relaxation withdrawn from it.

Try the above exercise with any part of your body, while lying on your back on a hard bed or on a blanket on the floor. When you relax your forearm or upper arm, be sure to let your arm hang loosely by your side and do not lift it up.

In lifting your arm you have to tense the muscles that raise your arm.

The purpose of tension and relaxation is to dissociate life force and mind from the consciousness of the body. When that is accomplished, the will and life force actually *own* the whole body and can, through their healing rays, remove chronic defects from any body part.

The Yogoda Exercises

Editor's note: Yogananda began to teach the Yogoda Exercises in 1918 at his boys' school in Ranchi, India. In his lessons in the 1920s he shared the exercises given below and in the Appendix. In the decades following, he developed them into a complete system of 39 exercises for recharging every part of the body, and called them the Energization Exercises. Yogananda considered his Energization Exercises a fundamental technique of the Kriya Yoga path.

If you are interested in learning the complete system of exercises, contact Crystal Clarity Publishers. The exercises are available in DVD, CD, poster, and booklet formats. The exercises in this book are a small fraction of the system that was later fully developed by the Master.

The Yogoda System constitutes an epoch-making discovery in the science of physical and inner culture.

The word Yogoda is derived from "Yoga," meaning harmony or equilibrium, and "da," that which imparts. Hence "Yogoda" means that system which imparts harmony and equilibrium to all the forces and faculties working for the perfection of body, mind, and soul.

Yogoda supplements and completes other systems of exercises, revolutionizing previous ideas of the evolution of bodily tissues and mental faculties. Through the right exercise of will, Yogoda resurrects dying tissue cells and worn out mental faculties, and helps form billions of new cells. Through Yogoda, all the various tissues—such as bone, muscle, connective, nerve, and adipose—are proportionately formed. Circulation, respiration, digestion, and all other involuntary processes of the body are harmonized and invigorated, and the mind is clarified.

Yogoda will be found to be the surest and most effective remedy for bodily diseases and inharmonious conditions of the mind. It acts as a healing balm for nervous abnormalities, stomach and abdominal troubles. It cures constipation by accelerating the peristaltic action of the intestinal muscles and quickening the secretions of the liver, pancreas, etc. It cures headaches, gout, and rheumatism by regulating the circulation; it eliminates colds and bronchitis by properly exercising the air cells. Brain power and memory are increased through greater blood supply. It raises the general vitality, resulting in the wonderful development of tissue strength and nerve vigor, thereby insuring greater longevity.

Yogoda teaches the art of consciously sending the curative life force to any diseased body part.

Once Yogoda is learned, ten minutes' daily practice will give results unequalled by those of most other forms of exercise. It avoids the bad effects of some other systems, such as exhaustion of the heart and other organs, and failure to give all-round development. It helps one detach the scattered attention from the senses and restless habits, and concentrate on one thing at a time.

Exercises with apparatus, such as dumb-bells, are mechanical. They lack the full, active involvement of the will, and so they do not give a feeling of ease and smooth flow but produce shocks in the system.

Since we often do not know the exact strength of our muscles and nerves, when we begin to use apparatus indiscriminately we can injure our nervous systems and muscles. When we perform exercises absent-mindedly, the will is denied the chance to prepare muscles to accept the exercises.

Do you want strength or do you want health? You answer, "I want both." But remember: too much attention given to gaining strength will make you miss real health—for the heart, lungs, and other vital organs can be overworked and thus weakened, just as when a motor is overworked. Yogoda will give wonderful health, vim, vigor, a feeling of freshness in every tissue, and more than sufficient strength.

A person may have cultivated great strength in his limbs, but he may not have good health. It is a mistake to suppose that physical exercises have for their sole object the attainment of strength. There are other tissues and organs in the human system besides the muscular. The healthy action of the lungs and stomach is far more important than great strength in the arms, legs, or back. It is foolish to cultivate strength of muscle alone while neglecting the important organs, and especially the will, which vivifies them all.

Yogoda Is Based on Eternal Truths

Yogoda is both a method of cure and a method of prevention of disease, mental weakness, and suffering. It is based on truth, corroborated by experience and strengthened by persistence.

Yogoda prevents hardening of the arteries and insures lasting youth by stimulating an even circulation and helping to eject foreign matter from the system. It revives, enlarges, and strengthens tissues; awakens lazy muscles; forms osseous or bony tissues; and accelerates involuntary functions such as those of the heart, lungs, stomach and intestines, capillaries, lymphatic glands, veins, and brain. Ordinarily we have no direct control over circulation, digestion, and other involuntary processes of the body. But we can influence them by the exercise of voluntary muscles over which we do have control.

Yogoda teaches how to surround each body cell with a ring of super-charged electrical vital energy and thus keep cells free from decay or bacterial invasion. Yogoda spiritualizes the body cells, converting them into undying soul and electrical life force.

An Inexhaustible Supply of Life Energy

Mental unwillingness always brings a lack of bodily energy, while willingness always brings a fresh supply of energy. From these facts we see the subtle relationship between energy and will power.

The special psychophysical technique of Yogoda enables one to connect the specific life current existing in the medulla oblongata with the Cosmic Life Energy that surrounds and permeates the body, thus insuring an inexhaustible supply.

Never say, "I am tired." Work willingly. As you work, feel the eternal energy flowing in you ceaselessly.

Each person wishes to be great in his own field, but often he cannot realize his wish. Why? Because people have no control over their bodies. Yogoda enables one to scientifically control all parts of the body, limbs, muscles, vocal organs, etc. Yogoda keeps muscles and tissues and the whole body disciplined, awake, and ever ready to act according to the directions of the Emperor Will.

Yogoda is the result of years of research and experiment. It is entirely simple and practicable; it is quickly learned and easily applied. Its effects are vital and "upbuilding" to a degree hitherto unknown. As Yogoda becomes known and practiced, it is bound to prove one of the greatest boons ever conferred on mankind.

Practicing the Exercises

Students should remember that the Yogoda exercises are to be done slowly at first, gently and rhythmically, never jerkily. Every movement must be harmonious. If any part of the body is especially weak, send the energy very slowly and gently, using only low tension. That body part will gradually be strengthened. By intensity of effort you can heal yourself very soon, since Yogoda gives you the power to draw the curative source, Cosmic Life Energy, into contact with diseased tissues. You can feel the actual current of energy being switched on in your body, wherever you want it. The vibration that you feel in a muscle is not voluntary movement; it is caused by the charge of energy into the body.

Under all circumstances, keep the spine straight and the body upright. Yogoda will give you grace and freedom of movement for dancing, swimming, wrestling, and walking. Most of all, it will teach you that you are not the body, that it is only your servant, and that you are the immortal Life Energy.

Exercise very slowly, willingly, and pleasantly, with eyes closed. By keeping the eyes closed concentration is keener, and energy currents are prevented from escaping through the eyes. More than one or two repetitions of any exercise are unnecessary if the above rule is observed. Practice regularly upon arising and whenever tired.

When performing the exercises, keep your mind on the medulla and imagine the energy flowing into your body through the medulla and from there to every part of the body. By keeping your mind thus fixed on the medulla, you will soon learn to draw in energy from the ether and send it to all parts of your body at will, without the physical process of tensing and relaxing. Always hold the thought, "I am calmly active; I am actively calm. I am the Prince of Peace sitting on the throne of poise."

Close your eyes and concentrate on the medulla. Feeling or visualizing the light there, repeat: "Thy cosmic current flows in me, flows in me, through my medulla flows in me, flows in me. I think and will the current to flow, in all my body the current to flow. I am charged, I am cured, I am charged, I am cured. Lightning flash goes through me. I am cured, I am cured."

First Exercise

1. Gently tense and relax each body part from 1 to 20, mentally saying: "My children, wake up." Place the attention in the center of the muscle and slowly tense the body part with low, medium, and high tension. Relax slowly and completely. Tense and then relax (from 1 to 20) left foot, right foot, left calf, right calf, left thigh, right thigh, left hip, right hip, abdomen (below navel), stomach (above navel), left forearm, right forearm, left upper arm, right upper arm, left breast, right breast, left of neck, right of neck, front of neck, back of neck, in slow rhythmic succession.

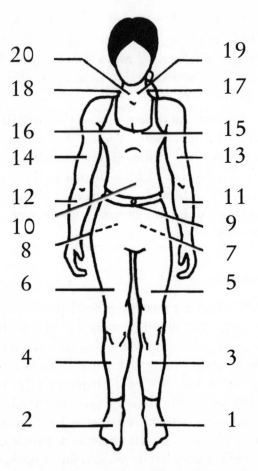

Tensing of the 20 body parts

hausted battery is recharged from a dynamo, so the holding of tension in any body part recharges that part. Hold the thought that God's electrical energy is flowing through you, and connect your will power with God's energy in your body.

Practice healing of any body part lying down. You can also do this standing, but when standing you have to keep certain muscles of the feet, calves, and thighs engaged in order to hold the body upright.

To remove pain in arm or leg, or to strengthen a limb: contract the limb gently with deep attention during exhalation, counting 1 to 20, then relax and inhale. Repeat six times, every morning and whenever necessary.

For strengthening knees: While exhaling, quickly squat to a sitting position balanced on toes, spine erect. Quickly stand up and inhale. Hold breath, and gently contract the whole body, then exhale and relax. Repeat ten times morning and night.

Throat exercise for getting rid of colds and for stimulating the vocal cords: With mouth closed roll your tongue backwards and forwards. Practice four times. Then put chin on chest and tense the front of the neck. Then lift chin upward with tension, relax and drop chin to chest. Repeat once.

For headaches: Very lightly press one palm on the back of the head and the other palm on the forehead. Inhale, hold breath, and gently contract the top of head with deep attention. Then exhale and release contraction of the top of head. During headaches, repeat four to six times as required.

For increasing brain power: Exhale and hold breath out. Contract the muscles of the head gently, holding full concentration there, counting 1 to 5. Inhale and release contraction of head. Repeat six times.

For strengthening the nerves: Inhale and hold breath. Gently tense the entire body all at once and hold the tension, counting 1 to 20, focusing with deep attention on the entire body. Exhale and release tension. Remain still, and enjoy the calmness of the body. Repeat three times a day, or any time you feel weak and nervous.

For strengthening the eyes: Exhale and hold breath out. Close your eyes, contracting the eyelids and brows very lightly. Hold contraction of eyes, with concentration, counting 1 to 20, then release contraction of eyelids. Inhale. Repeat seven times, morning and night.

ॐ ॐ ॐ

Affirmation to Practice after All Yogoda Exercises

O Eternal Energy!
Awaken within me conscious will,
conscious vitality, conscious health.
Good will to all, vitality to all, good health to all.

O Eternal Energy!
By Thy Power I know that in tension
I put forth energy into the body
and in relaxation I withdraw it.
I am a tenant in the body sent here by Thy Grace
to rule it, but never to be identified with it.

O Eternal Energy!
Impart to me spiritual patience
that I may regularly practice the exercises
both morning and night
to the best of my ability.

Eternal youth of body and mind, abide in me
forever, forever, forever!
My mind, awake! Sleep no more, awake!
Sleep no more, wake, sleep no more!
Peace! Peace! Peace!

I am strong, I am strength, I am healthy, I am health,
I am successful, I am success,
I am blessed, I am bliss, I am peaceful, I am peace,
I am Immortal, I am Immortality.

Peace, Bliss, Peace!

∼✺∼

More Affirmations and Prayers for Divine Energy

O Spirit, teach me to heal the body by recharging it
with Thy Cosmic Energy, to heal the mind
by concentration and smiles, to heal the soul
by meditation-born intuition.
Make me feel that my heart is throbbing in Thy breast,
and that Thou art walking through my feet,
breathing through my breath, wielding my
arms of activity, and weaving thoughts in my brain.
O, make me Thyself, that I may behold
the little bubble of me, floating in Thee!

∼✺∼

Beloved God, charge my body with Thy vitality.
Charge my mind with Thy spiritual power.
Charge my soul with Thy joy, with Thine immortality.
Through Self-realization within me, I will find
the emancipation that leads to Thee.

✧

I live, move, and have my being in Spirit,
as a fish lives in the water, and a bird in the air.
I will consciously draw strength, health, and happiness
from this all-enveloping Presence.

✧

O Conscious Cosmic Energy,
Thou alone dost directly support my body.
Solid, liquid, and gaseous foods are converted
and spiritualized into energy by Thy Cosmic Energy.
Help me to learn, O Spirit, to live more and more
by direct Cosmic Energy, and less and less by food.
Thine energy burns in the bulb of my five senses.
I recharge myself with Thine omnipresent, Cosmic Energy.

✧

I will life force to charge,
With Godly will I will it charge
Through my nerves and muscles all,
My tissues, limbs, and all.
With vibrant tingling fire,
With burning joyous power,
In blood and glands,
By sovereign command,
I bid you flow.
By my command
I bid you glow,
By my command
I bid you glow.

⌎⌏

Let me feel that Thou art the electricity of my life,
which moves the machinery of my
bones, nerves, and muscles.
In every heartthrob, every breath,
every outburst of vital activity,
teach me to feel Thy Power.

ॐ ॐ ॐ

Rejuvenation means to live fully and to feel youthful to the end of your days. You must learn how to rejuvenate the body not only through proper diet but through Life Energy, by developing will power. You can bring energy into the body by will power. Each one of you can rejuvenate yourself. When your body becomes recharged from the Infinite Source, then you will learn to smile from your soul.

Behind your body wave is the vast ocean of God; behind your soul is the wisdom of God; behind your mind is the great intelligence of God. Attuning yourself with Him, you will know that you are the child of God.

Chapter 2

All-Round Healthy Living

True Health

Health does not mean mere existence. Keeping out of the hospital is not health. To be able to resist disease, to bear strain, to stimulate mental vitality, and to feel the body as a luxury—as a bird feels when shooting through the air, and as a child does always—is health.

The Magnetic Diet

What distilled water is to a wet battery, food is to the body battery. The Life Energy in the body battery is derived from Cosmic Energy through the medulla, and from food. It is the intricate task of the life force to distill additional life force from the nourishment taken into the body, by breaking up foods and converting them into energy. Therefore, one's diet should be confined to foods that are easily converted into energy. Oxygen and sunshine should have a very important place in people's lives, because of their direct energy-producing quality.

The more you depend on the will and on Cosmic Energy to sustain you, the less your food requirements; the more you depend on food, the weaker your will and the less your recourse to Cosmic Energy.

The magnetic diet consists of such food substitutes as sunrays and oxygen, which can be easily assimilated and converted into energy. Magnetic foods give energy more quickly than solids and liquids, which are less easily converted into life force.

When you are tired or hungry, take a sunbath and you will find yourself revived and recharged with ultraviolet rays. Inhale and exhale several times outdoors or near an open window, and your fatigue will be gone. A fasting person who inhales and exhales deeply twelve times, three times a day, recharges his body with electrons and free energy from air and ether.

Practice the following exercise three times a day: Exhale slowly, counting from 1 to 6. Now, while the lungs are empty, mentally count from 1 to 6. Inhale slowly, counting from 1 to 6. Then hold the breath, counting from 1 to 6. Repeat eleven times.

Just as electricity passing through a rod made of a conductive substance electrifies it, so life force derived from oxygen charges the body battery. People who perform breathing exercises always have shining, magnetic eyes.

Each one of the many billions of cells within the human body is a tiny mouth taking nourishment. The life force identified with the body creates within us a desire to derive energy from meat and other foods taken into the stomach. The life force must be trained to draw energy from subtler sources. The body's energy requirements can be supplied partly by sunshine and oxygen, which are absorbed by the pores. For this reason, the surface of the skin must be kept scrupulously clean at all times.

The Mental Diet

We must also remember that good thoughts are nourishing food for the mind, and thoughts of any other nature are poisonous to the body and mind.

Have you ever analyzed your mental diet? It consists of the thoughts you think as well as the thoughts you receive from close thought-contact with your friends. Peaceful thoughts and peaceful friends always produce healthy, magnetic minds. Inner disquietude and worries, due to the wrong sort of friends or unappreciative relatives, produces an unwholesome, gloomy mind.

If you are suffering from mental ill health, go on a mental diet. A health-giving mental fast will clear the mind and rid it of the accumulated mental poisons from a careless, faulty mental diet.

First of all, learn to remove the causes of your worries without permitting them to worry you. Do not feed your mind with mental poisons of fresh worries created daily.

Worries are often the result of attempting to do too many things hurriedly. Do not "bolt" your mental duties, but thoroughly masticate them one at a time with the teeth of attention, and saturate them with the saliva of good judgment. Thus will you avoid worry indigestion.

Acquiring Physical, Mental, and Spiritual Perfection

Eating spiritual, magnetism-producing foods and absorbing vitality-producing sunshine daily, you will physically reflect God's everlasting youth. Eliminating all mental poisons and partaking of the divine nourishment of determination, courage, and continuous mental effort and concentration, you will learn to overcome the most difficult problems with ease. Eliminating ignorance by constant meditation on God and following the precepts of Yogoda and your spiritual teacher, you will attain perfect spiritual health.

Once you learn to eat right foods, think right thoughts, and be filled with wisdom and joy, your body and mind will be spiritualized and experienced as dynamos of magnetic energy. Your body and mind, purified by this energy, will take on the beauty of the Spirit, and be a spiritual magnet, charged with the life of God, blessing all those it touches.

ళ ళ ళ

How to Remain Youthful

The careful man who follows health laws suffers rarely compared with the careless man who does not discriminate about his diet. Walk daily. Bathe your body in the bacteria-killing sunshine every day. When winter and its healthful outdoor sports are here, take time to go skating, skiing, and walking. Breathe the fresh, crisp, invigorating air of winter. By these means, disease will be dispelled.

You must take care of your body machine. As the years roll along, do not give up—as so many people do. Always be interested. Keep the mind busy creating new things. The infinite powers are at your command.

The ocean can help any wave to retain its form if it keeps pushing it from within its bosom. So man can retain youth by asking the everlasting ocean of Immortal Power behind the wave of his body to continue manifesting itself as that youthful, vital form.

ళ ళ ళ

Using AUM for Healing

Concentrate the mind on any weak or diseased part. As you mentally chant "AUM" fifteen times in that body part, try to feel that a warm electric force is filling it with healing energy.

ॐ ॐ ॐ

Bathe in God's Sunlight

When the sun shines, everything seems to smile with its halo of golden rays. Sunlight and ultraviolet ray baths are necessary to fill the tissues and pores with life-giving energy. They redden the hemoglobin, recharging it and making it richer and healthier. As an ordinary bath washes away bacteria and dirt from the human body, so the ultraviolet rays in sunlight cleanse the body of bacteria. Ultraviolet rays penetrate the homes of enemy bacteria in the fingernails and body pores, and scorch them out.

If you do not have time for a walk, open your windows and let your life-giving friend, Sunlight, fall on you and bathe you all over. If you are afraid of catching cold, jump up and down to stay warm, but each morning bathe in the ocean of sunrays that God has created for you.

ॐ ॐ ॐ

Filling the Body with Energy

While walking every day, slowly inhale counting 1 to 12. Hold the breath for twelve counts, then exhale while counting 1 to 12. Do this twenty-four times every time you go for a walk.

Take sunbaths as often as you can, from ten minutes to one-half hour, according to the strength of the sun. Do not overdo this. Be careful of severe sunburn, which does more harm than good. (The amount of time for sun bathing should be gradually built up to one-half hour, and regulated according to your skin's tolerance for sun rays.)

Bathing in sunlight-heated or ultraviolet-ray-saturated water is very beneficial.

Rubbing the whole stripped body vigorously and rapidly with the palms before taking a bath generates life force and is very beneficial.

Occasionally holding on to two electrodes of a battery is a good method for supplying the body with free energy. (The electric current should be very weak.)

If a weak man lives in the same room with a strong person, he absorbs some of the latter's vital and mental magnetism. For this reason, young and old people should mingle and thus exchange magnetism.

Try to discover new methods for drawing more energy and magnetism into the body.

ॐ ॐ ॐ

Ingredients of Health

After school days, the days of exercise are usually over and the days of over-eating and its resultant sickness begin. Many people do not realize that uniform health depends on:

- proper eating
- fasting
- proper exercise
- fresh air and sunbaths
- good thoughts and cheerfulness

- less eating
- conservation of vital energy by self-control
- proper elimination
- calm meditation

ॐ ॐ ॐ

How to Fall Asleep

Sleep can be induced at will by lying on the back, closing the eyes, tensing and relaxing the body, and dismissing all thoughts. Try this until you learn to sleep or dream at will. With closed eyes, visualize a different room from the one in which you are resting, and fall asleep thinking of it. In this manner dreams can be induced.

ॐ ॐ ॐ

For Healthy Teeth

Why disobey God's little laws that govern the body beautiful? You take your lunch, give your lips a hasty napkin rub, and rush out feeling that everything is all right. But what about your teeth—why deny them a cleansing shower bath after they have worked so hard for you? Diseased teeth produce many ills. The Hindu pundits say to rinse your mouth with water ten times after each meal if you have no toothbrush handy.

ॐ ॐ ॐ

Healthy Living

Besides exercise, pure air, sunshine, and right eating, the rules for happy, healthy living include the mental habits of heartfelt smiles, creative activity, concentration, good character, and keeping good company.

Keep yourself mentally disinfected by the strong faith that nothing can harm you, that you are always protected.

Chapter *3*

Food for Health of Body, Mind, and Soul

Right Attitude Toward Diet

We must strike a balance between non-attachment to outer things and sensible concern for our present realities. So long as a person is centered in body-consciousness, he must take sensible care of his body. It is important spiritually, also, to take reasonable physical precautions. Proper diet, proper exercise, fresh air, and sunlight: These things are necessary for a well-rounded existence.

Make God, not food, your religion. Many faddists only weaken their systems by depending excessively on dietary principles. "Oh!" they'll cry, "I didn't get my avocado to-day; my spine feels weak!" That very preoccupation with secondary matters only weakens their will power. Their very attitude toward life becomes spineless! Such concern for su-perficialities is like working to seal the cracks in a plaster wall when termites are eating away at the foundation!

ॐ ॐ ॐ

The Value of Natural Foods

If the stimulation of Life Energy is responsible for man's well-being, why is food so important? All cells, including those in the food we eat, have latent intelligence and can influence our mind and brain cells. Natural foods like raw fruits, vegetables, and nuts have a harmonious and strengthening effect on the mind and permit the Life Energy to flow unimpeded through the body.

Meat, which retains the vibrations of the pain, fear, and anger of the dying animal, and denatured foods are irritating and disturbing to the equilibrium of the mind, which is thus robbed of its birthright of power to direct Life Energy to heal any part of the body. While food itself cannot heal, natural foods indirectly produce health by keeping the mind calm, thus permitting the Life Energy to flow unobstructed.

ॐ ॐ ॐ

Magnetism and Right Diet

In order to have magnetism, keep your body free from poisons. If your body is filled with poisons, your energy is more or less bound up. Try to clean out those poisons. If you are clean within, then all your energy can be displayed through your eyes, your face, and your body. You must pay attention to your diet. Raw food produces magnetism. Coconut produces lots of magnetism. Beets, spinach, and lettuce are full of vitality and give you magnetism.

Too much meat causes you to lose your magnetism because animal magnetism tampers with your spiritual magnetism. Meat causes you to concentrate on the physical plane too much, and you tend to attract physical companions instead of spiritual ones. Meat also over-stimulates sexual desire. If you eat a little bit of meat it won't hurt you, but if you make a habit of eating it daily, it will destroy your magnetic qualities. Eat good meat substitutes, including more nuts and nutmeat combinations.

Too much starchy food and protein retains the poisons in the body. Eating freely of fruits and vegetables can help you develop magnetism. Fruits are even more magnetized than vegetables. They are filled with sunshine and vital energy. Overeating is bad. Fasting is very good, as it gives the stomach a rest. Your eyes and your whole body will be magnetized by the kind of food you eat.

ॐ ॐ ॐ

Faith and Dietary Laws

To have faith in God's healing power through the mind and to *obey* dietary laws is better than just to have faith in God and mental power and to *disregard* dietary laws.

ॐ ॐ ॐ

Diet and Disposition

Our diet affects our state of mind either favorably or unfavorably, and whatever affects our state of mind affects our disposition. It is necessary to eat the proper food in order to make a proper brain as well as a proper body. All food has some effect on the mind.

The human machine is not unlike an automobile or a steam engine. The efficiency of mechanical engines is largely dependent on the fuel supplied to them; similarly, the condition of the human machine is largely dependent on the food that a person eats. Food has much to do with developing such things as character, ability, and social habits.

It is desirable to know not only the physical but also the spiritual and psychological effects of food. The three psychological qualities of food:

SATTWIC — develops moral and spiritual qualities

RAJASIC — develops active and worldly qualities

TAMASIC — increases darkening or deadening qualities

Sattwic foods include fruits, vegetables, whole grains and legumes, honey, fresh dairy products, coconut milk, peanut and almond pastes, and nuts. These foods produce calmness and nobility.

Rajasic foods are those that produce active, worldly, strong, and emotional qualities of the mind. These foods include onions, garlic, eggs, horseradish, pumpkin, potatoes, pickles, and spices, as well as fish, fowl, and lamb.

Tamasic foods have darkening, destructive qualities. Foods that are full of odor, putrefied, or artificially made (deprived of their natural qualities) are tamasic. Examples are Roquefort cheese, cold storage foods, and liquors, as well as beef, veal, and pork. These foods produce pride, jealousy, greed, and vengefulness.

Some spiritual qualities of food are:

NUTS: Help deep thinking, good for brain power and concentration.

FRUITS: Develop heart and spiritual qualities.

VEGETABLES: Give power of management over the body.

CEREALS: Produce strength of character.

MILK AND EGGS: Give enthusiasm, fresh energy.

CERTAIN FRUITS: peaches, selflessness; grapes, spiritual love; banana, humility; strawberry, dignity; pineapple, courage; cherries, cheerfulness.

ॐ ॐ ॐ

Building the Body Temple

Every day the tissues must be supplied with proper body-building materials. In plastering a house, if you mix less lime in the sand, at first you may not notice anything wrong with the looks of the plaster, but in a short time the plaster will begin to fall off. Similarly, our bodies decay when not "plastered" with the right kind of blood containing the right kind and quantity of body-building elements. The body begins to lose vigor, the tissues become flabby, the skin begins to wrinkle, and the cells begin to lose their building power. So, in arranging your breakfast, lunch, and dinner, be sure you are giving the body the proper food substances.

ॐ ॐ ॐ

Vitamins Are the Brains of Your Food

Experiments show that mice can live eight weeks on water alone, but only six weeks on white bread. Without the presence of vitamins in food, your meal is dead. Instead of nourishing yourself, you invite disease.

Diseases are born of our ignorance of the laws of the body and mind. Right eating, moderation, and exercise will practically banish disease from the face of the earth. Vitamins are the brains of the food you eat. They direct the digestion and absorption of food and the building of various tissues. Vitamins are condensed life force. They are subtle electricity stored in food to replete the body battery with fresh energy. Do not eat vitamin-killed boiled dinners. Without vitamins, the swallowed food goes into the stomach without direction.

One should not have a starvation meal or eat less than one needs of the right foods. A man of sedentary habits, such as a writer or an office worker, should eat small quantities several times a day rather than a few large meals a day; he should fast occasionally. A man doing physical labor should eat more, including meat substitutes, nuts, and milk.

ॐ ॐ ॐ

Let Hunger Be Your Guide

Eating three meals a day is a dangerous habit. Many are led to their graves quickly because they eat at the sound of the dinner bell. Ignore its ominous call if you are not hungry. It is good to eat at a regular time because a psychological expectancy is created in the body cells, which helps the secretion of digestive juices. The intelligent cells, like hungry animals at the zoo, wait for the dinner hour.

But never eat unless you are hungry. Eat moderately if you are hungry. Eat less if you are a little hungry. Eat nothing if you are not hungry at all. Omit the meals that you would try to eat with little hunger, and this will sharpen your hunger for the next meal. Use your will power to resist the temptation of eating three meals every day, which keeps the whole system—including the cells, heart, nerves, and stomach—working continuously. Give your intelligent machine occasional rest by eliminating breakfast, lunch, or dinner. If you are working hard and are very hungry, you may safely eat three light meals daily, but if you don't do much manual labor then two meals a day are plenty.

ॐ ॐ ॐ

Eat Lightly

This body has been given to enable you to accomplish certain works on the material plane; you should take care of it as your most precious possession. There is a Syrian proverb, "The enemy of man is his stomach." Overloading the stomach with unnecessary food is one of the most common abuses of the body. Eat sparingly and notice the great change in your health for the better.

ॐ ॐ ॐ

Develop Won't Power

If you haven't enough will power, try to develop "won't" power. When you are at the dinner table and Mr. Greed lures you to eat more than you should and tries to chloroform your self-control and cast you into the pit of indigestion, watch yourself. After partaking of the right quantity and quality of food, say to yourself, "I won't eat any more," and get up from the table and run. When somebody calls, "John, come back and eat some more. Don't forget the delicious apple pie," just call back, "I won't."

ॐ ॐ ॐ

Eating Properly

Important considerations in eating and digesting food are:

1. Proper selection of food
2. Attractive appearance and aroma
3. Pleasant environment

Food should not be eaten under the stress of emotion. There should be only calmness and pleasantness at meal time; all adverse thoughts and emotions should be put aside. One should partake of food with a thankful, joyful heart.

ॐ ॐ ॐ

Meat Eating versus Vegetarianism

The question of meat eating and vegetarianism is a complicated and controversial subject. What I say will be governed by present world needs.* I believe that no absolute view can be given which is good for all times and all people.

Our conscience and human sensitiveness are roused much more by the killing of animals than by the slaughtering of vegetables and the skinning of fruits. Most steak eaters would not eat beef if they had to kill to get their meat, but no vegetarian would mind chopping off the heads of carrots. The spilling of blood and administering of pain in killing animals shows that the animals are approaching nearer to human beings in the scale of evolution.

Meat is concentrated food and is strengthening, but it is highly constipating, a retainer of body poisons, and a harbinger of disease. Vegetables and fruits, having a natural laxative action, are conducive to health and to the elimination of diseases. Vegetables have to be eaten with more patience and are not as concentrated as meat; the improper eating of vegetables does not produce strength.

Americans are suffering from obesity due to eating an over-abundance of various forms of proteins, such as meat, milk, and nuts. Americans should become vegetarians.

* Written in 1935.

Meat-eating races are usually politically free. Vegetarian India has not been strong enough to dispel continuous foreign aggressions. Hindus have almost no protein to eat, and due to fanaticism they indulge in a starch-predominant diet, and therefore die thin and early in life. Animals live longer than human beings in India.

As a temporary measure, present-day India needs to eat lamb, goat, and fowl until she can get enough milk or meat substitutes. Lamb has been found to agree better with the chemical elements in man's body than any other form of meat.

Man's life is more valuable to all living creatures than is the life of animals. If the choice must be made whether man should eat meat in order to live, or whether the animals should live and man should die without eating meat, I would say that man should live at the expense of the animal.

We find that both vegetarians and meat eaters have lived long and healthy lives. Jesus, Buddha, and St. Francis ate meat; Shankara, Chaitanya, and some great Christ-like saints of India did not eat meat. Saint Peter was shown a vision of some animals and asked to kill them and eat. "Thou shalt not kill" was meant to apply to people and not to animals. Moses and Jesus both ate meat, and Moses was the giver of the Ten Commandments.

Fish have blood and a nervous system, but very few fish make any noise when they are killed. Life evolves more complex forms in the mammals, which have different tissues from the fish. The bull and hog, having highly developed, pugnacious nervous systems, feel greater pain and they loudly protest any attempt to kill them. These animals have evolved enough consciousness to understand the love of self-preservation and the injustice of inflicting pain, and therefore they should not be killed. The lamb protests less violently than the bull or hog.

It looks as if the vegetables, fish, and meek animals are intentionally given by Nature a less developed nervous system that does not register much pain or evoke reactionary protests during pain. This may be one reason why these lower forms of life are made to sacrifice their lives for the maintenance of the higher forms of life.

ॐ ॐ ॐ

Live in Joy

Remember, it is not only what goes into you but what comes out of you that makes you what you are. Some people who eat meat may be holy and self-controlled, and some who eat only vegetables and fruits may be knaves and lead uncontrolled lives. Above all, eat rightly, think rightly, meditate, and live in Divine Joy, night and day.

৺ ৺ ৺

Don't Be Fanatical

You must remember to follow the God-made material laws that govern your health and physical body. But do not over-emphasize the importance of the body nor be too fastidious about diet, because mind-power is more essential. There are food "cranks" whose only interest revolves around calories and vitamins, and they talk of nothing but lettuce and nuts, lettuce and nuts, until you wonder how they can be so blind to other, more interesting aspects of life.

But don't misunderstand me. I am not underestimating the value of a proper diet. I simply point out that it is better not to become fanatical about it.

৺ ৺ ৺

Affirm Divine Freedom

The soul is independent of food. The body should also express this freedom of the soul. Food seems to be the greatest bondage of the soul to the body.

Affirm: "Good food, any kind of food, or no food at all are alike to me because my body emanates from my soul, which is unconditioned, and I am above food, hunger, and decay. I am immortal, I am satisfied, all my wants are fulfilled. I am above hunger, decay, or death."

Chapter *4*

Selection of a Correct Diet

Chapter 4

Selection of a Correct Diet

A Vegetarian Diet

To my first generation of students, I didn't say much about a vegetarian diet: it was too unusual, then, for the people in this country.* Diet was secondary in importance, anyway, to the teachings of yoga.

For the next generation, I recommended that they eat less meat. Most of them, on an average, became healthier.

For this third generation, I've recommended a completely vegetarian diet, and find that, of the three groups, the present one is the most healthy.

I don't care much, however, for that word, "vegetarian." Too many people are fanatics on the subject. I've coined what I consider a better word: "propereatarian."

ళ ళ ళ

Balanced Living

Obey the material laws of the body by a sensible choice of food. Since you have to eat, eat the right kind of food. Choose a balanced diet, stick to it, and then forget the body; devote your time to the more important studies and problems of life.

* Yogananda came to the United States in 1920.

❦ ❦ ❦

How to Embrace a Healthier Diet

Often I am informed, "Oh, asthma (or tuberculosis or diabetes) runs in the family." I do not need to be further told of their self-hypnotic resignation to an identical doom. But this, dear students, is NOT the way to Truth; it is a jellyfish philosophy. What IS true, is that if you continue to live as did your father who died of cancer, you may expect to follow in his footsteps.

I do not maintain that it is easy to change—like everything else worth attaining, you must work for it! But there is a saying that "any old fish can float downstream, but it takes a *live* one to swim upstream." It is the individual's job to free himself from the shackles of undesirable hereditary tendencies, whether habits of thought, or habits of ill health.

If my words are finding fertile soil in your mind, take inventory of your own situation, rearrange your life, change your habits of living, and keep step with your ever-changing spiritual understanding and developing mental power.

Do bacon and eggs, coffee, corned beef hash, white sugar, hot dogs, hamburgers, condiments, white flour products, liquor, tobacco, and the rest of the lifeless, devitalized, acid-forming, low-vibrating food imitations still form the coals with which you fuel the embers of your bloodstream? If so, then you are tenaciously clutching yesterday's tools of ignorance, afraid to exchange the ox-cart for motor power.

Are you ready to change your diet?

For a person in good health, the day's diet should be divided into 60% fruits and vegetables, 20% protein, and 20% starches and sugar. Let us imagine that we have before us two plates: The large dinner plate, whose duty heretofore has been to be served chock-full of concentrated, acid-forming, "good, solid, nourishing foods"; and half the size of the large plate, the smaller one is able to hold a lonesome lettuce leaf and a slice of tomato, answering to the name of "salad."

Now, let's switch about and build the meal around the salad, filling the large plate with live, high-vibrating, colorful sources of minerals and vitamins, such as green lettuce, watercress, parsley, spinach, green and red peppers, celery, tomatoes, and cabbage. On the small plate we will have any of the concentrated foods chosen from among: meat (lamb or chicken, but not pork or beef), fish, dairy products, eggs, nuts, legumes (dried lentils, peas, beans, garbanzos), mushrooms, or soybeans. Sample serving sizes: from 10 to 15 nuts may be considered an adult portion; 4 ounces of meat; a little more than 4 ounces of fish; 2 eggs.

ॐ ॐ ॐ

Properly Combining Foods

To obtain the best results from your food, carefully consider how to properly combine the items eaten at one meal and reduce them to the very minimum. The fewer different foods used at one meal, especially if one has any digestive difficulties, the better. Even of fruits, it is well to use but one at a time. In fact, frequent meals composed of only one fruit are an excellent idea. Try eating, for example, all the apples you wish and nothing else for your lunch. They are filling, satisfying, and have much food value, as well as being an important source of sodium, the alkalinizing chemical. Or, you might try grapes, oranges, or any other fruit you prefer.

While the body does require various types of food for harmonious balance, it is impossible to handle them all at one sitting. In the beginning, healthy cells have selective intelligence and possess the faculty of choosing what they need and avoiding what they cannot utilize. In most cases, due to years of ignorant disregard for their normal requirements, the cells have lost that power of selection, as have the taste buds in the mouth.

Could you follow a musical score, read, walk, write, talk, and meditate simultaneously, doing justice to them all? Well, that is just about what the digestive organs are called on to do three times a day, year in and year out, with an incompatible conglomeration of food-stuffs tossed into their apparatus—a marvelous machine, which no mechanical reproductions have yet equaled.

There are five separate digestive fluids in the body, designed to handle the variety of foods we need. In the mouth, the process of digestion of starches and sugars takes place. That is why it is important to thoroughly insalivate carbohydrates. In the stomach, proteins are taken care of. The bile manufactured by the liver and gall bladder takes care of the fats. The pancreatic juices assist in further digestion of the carbons, as well as the proteins and fats. The intestinal juices work on all the foods, preparing them for a more complete state of digestion and assimilation.

The confusion that takes place internally when too many different foods are foisted on an overtaxed "public servant" might be compared to that caused when the manager of a big manufacturing plant issues conflicting orders to the various departments.

When eyes and palate dictate how we nourish this physical temple, to the exclusion of the laws that *should* govern it, there is little wonder that our population fills an increasing number of hospitals, sanitariums, and asylums.

Do's:

- Use a mono-diet occasionally to give the vital organs a much needed rest.
- Combine proteins with fruits, vegetables, and fats.
- Combine vegetables with any foods.

Do not's:

- Do not use more than one starch at a meal.
- Do not use more than one protein at a meal. Example: fish and cheese, eggs and milk.
- Do not use starches and citrus fruits together. Example: lemonade and bread.
- Do not use proteins and starches at the same meal. Example: fish and bread; meat and bread.

Some good combinations:

- Buttermilk and dates
- Milk and fruit
- Vegetables and bread
- Fish and tomatoes, and other non-starchy vegetables

☺ ☺ ☺

Alkalinity for Health

The normal medium in which the body performs its functions is alkaline. When, as a result of improper diet, overwork, lack of rest, or lack of fresh air, the body becomes acid, we become ill. The alkalinity that the body needs at this time to neutralize the acid condition is supplied through food and drink. Alkalinity brings health and immunity to disease.

In order to keep the body in an alkaline condition, at least eighty per cent of our diet should be chosen from foods that have an alkaline reaction, such as tomatoes, lettuce, celery, watercress, cucumbers, beets, eggplant, spinach, asparagus, carrots, leeks, chard, squash, mushrooms, soy beans, strawberries, pears, figs, cantaloupes, oranges, peaches, lemons, raspberries, apricots, watermelons, apples, dates, grape juice, and buttermilk.

☺ ☺ ☺

Diet Suggestions

Fruit should be eaten with bread or some other starchy food, but without sugar; you may add a little honey if you wish. Eat only nature's candies (unsulphured figs, prunes, or raisins).

Do not eat too much white sugar. The ingestion of excessive quantities of sweets causes intestinal fermentation.

Remember, foods prepared from white flour, such as white bread and white-flour gravy, as well as polished rice and too many fried foods, are injurious to your health. White flour acts like glue and obstructs the expulsion of bodily waste materials. Rough food, like bran, is very good to free you of constipation. Remember, constipation is the most dangerous of all diseases.

Try to include in your daily diet as much raw food as possible. There are lots of energy-producing vitamins in all uncooked green vegetables. Cooking destroys the energy. Nature is the best cook. She prepares all vegetables and fruits with ultraviolet rays and distilled water. When you eat uncooked fruits and vegetables, all the energy and chemicals enter directly into your blood without being lost.

Eat some baked vegetables because you are accustomed to cooked vegetables, but learn to eat more unfired, Nature-cooked food for the proper maintenance of your body. If you cook vegetables, eat them with the juice in which they were boiled.

Drink at least a glassful of good milk each day. Milk is the only food except eggs that alone can support human life. Both the extreme "cooked-food lover" and the "raw-food faddist" often omit from their diets many elements needed for the proper building of the body. No matter what your views on food may be, you will be safe if you drink milk. It will help prevent old age and the sudden deterioration of the body, which result from not giving the body all the elements necessary for its healthy maintenance. Never drink milk with your meals. Milk taken with a heavy dinner produces indigestion. Drink milk alone or with fruits.

In preparing grains, steaming is far superior to boiling them, not only because of the improvement in taste and appearance, but for preserving the food value. Try such products as whole wheat cereals, steel cut oats, buckwheat or barley grits, brown rice, and dried corn, which are best secured at health food stores.

Eat very little meat—only chicken, lamb, and fish occasionally if you are used to eating meat and think your system demands it. Nuts, cottage cheese, eggs, milk, cream, coconuts, and bananas are very good meat and fish substitutes. If you eat chicken, lamb, or fish, have a vegetable salad with them.

Do not drink water with meals. This habit destroys the shape of the body. Eating too much at one meal, followed by lack of exercise, develops the body disproportionately.

It is easy to eat, lured by taste, but it will be hard to get rid of fat if you accumulate it through overeating and lack of exercise. The heart is kept in better condition when the body is thin. The less flesh, the less strain on the heart. Do not drink too much water or other liquids.

Eat less and chew well. Do not mix starchy foods with liquids (for example, eat no bread with milk), as liquids dilute the saliva required to assist digestion.

ॐ ॐ ॐ

Nuts

The best meat substitute is ground nuts. Nuts are a highly concentrated protein and should be eaten with discrimination as to amount and to other foods combined with them. They should be eaten in the earlier part of the day, as they require many hours for digestion.

Nuts should be taken in combination with fruits and vegetables rich in sodium, especially green leafy vegetables. Man's almost universal habit of eating too fast makes it hard for him to masticate nuts thoroughly enough before swallowing; therefore, it is better to grind up the nuts or eat them in the form of unroasted nut butters.

Nuts should never be used as a dessert after a heavy meal because they require the full action of the digestive juices. When taken after a heavy meal they may prove quite harmful, but when combined with fruits or vegetable salads, nuts make a complete meal in themselves.

ೞ ೞ ೞ

Fruits and Vegetables

Vegetables and fruits, having a natural laxative action, are conducive to health and to the elimination of diseases. All fruits are laxative in the following order: prunes, watermelons, cantaloupes, passion fruits, tomatoes, figs, raisins, and grapes.

The juice of one lemon or lime diluted in warm water, without sugar and drunk alone, is known to be very good for the liver, spleen, intestines, and kidneys. Lemon juice taken daily is known to disinfect the physical organs. The acid in the lemon destroys any undesirable germs that get into the body through food.

ೞ ೞ ೞ

The Daily Diet

Your daily food intake should be chosen from the following list of foods that contain all the elements needed for the proper maintenance of the body:

- ½ apple
- ¼ grapefruit
- 1 lemon
- 1 lime
- 1 orange
- 1 glass orange juice with a tablespoon of finely ground nuts
- 1 small piece fresh pineapple
- 6 figs, dates, or prunes
- 1 handful raisins
- 1 tsp. honey
- 1 baked, half-boiled, or steamed vegetable with its juice
- 1 raw carrot, including some of its green top
- 6 leaves raw spinach
- ¼ heart of lettuce
- 1 tsp. olive oil
- 1 glass milk
- ⅛ glass cream
- 1 tbsp. cottage cheese
- 1 tbsp. clabber

Eat at least some of the above foods every day, distributing them over your three meals. Omit those foods mentioned above which do not agree with you. Eat very lightly when you feel the need of nourishment, and gradually accustom yourself to a more wholesome diet. You may increase or decrease the quantities given above, in accordance with your individual needs. The person doing strenuous muscular work of course requires more food than the sedentary worker.

Whenever hungry, take a large tablespoonful of thoroughly ground nuts in half a glass of water or in a glass of orange juice. When thirsty, drink a glass of orange juice or water (preferably distilled or boiled). However, nature's distilled water—undiluted fruit juice—is best.

Ice water should be taken sparingly at any time, but especially during and after meals as it lowers the temperature of the stomach, thus retarding digestion. Never drink ice water when you are overheated.

A common blunder of vegetarians is to eat an insufficient amount or to eat a "dead meal" of over-cooked vegetables, minus all the vitamins. Eating meat is not worse than eating only a boiled disintegrated hash of vegetable corpses. By eating boiled vegetable dinners, vegetarians lose strength and inwardly want to go back to a meat diet.

Following this menu saves one the trouble of reading elaborate diet books, and prevents the sudden invasion of diseases arising from the omission of one or more of the sixteen elements and vitamins the body requires for sustenance.

ॐ ॐ ॐ

Prayer-Demand Before Taking Food

Heavenly Father, Receive this food. Make it holy. Let no impurity of greed defile it. The food comes from Thee. It is to build Thy temple. Spiritualize it. Spirit to Spirit goes. We are the petals of Thy manifestation, but Thou art the flower, its life, beauty, and loveliness. Permeate our souls with the fragrance of Thy presence.

Chapter 5

DIET FOR HEALING AND BEAUTY

Healing Methods

The first person ever to feel disease or discomfort in the body probably stopped eating, as do the animals. Therefore, the first method of healing is fasting, or giving rest to the human machinery. That original sick person must have been instinctively led to eliminate certain hard-to-digest foods from his diet and seek easy-to-digest roots or herbs. This led to the discovery of different herbs as medicine. The Chinese and Hindus have specialized in this second method of healing. Later, due to migration, change of climate, and difficulty in finding the required herbs on demand, concentrated extracts and medicines began to be made from herbs. Thus, the third method of healing was through herbal medicines.

ॐ ॐ ॐ

Curing Autointoxication

One of the main causes of arthritis, rheumatism, and many other diseases is autointoxication, which is due to faulty elimination. Uneliminated, decayed food stays like a paste on the walls of the intestines and is absorbed into the bloodstream. Disease naturally follows.

Progressive doctors are endorsing the plan of a fruit juice or water fast one day each week. Another sensible medical recommendation is to evacuate the intestines and flush the bowels completely once or twice a month by a day of drinking only vegetable juices or two or three quarts of water. This general housecleaning is helpful.

☙ ☙ ☙

Don't Drink Ice Water

Doctors say that ice cold water lowers the temperature of the stomach thirty degrees; then the stomach must warm up again to resume its normal activities. This is shocking and disastrous to the weak digestive power of an individual.

☙ ☙ ☙

Avoiding Colds

The man who eats without real physical hunger, but with pseudo-hunger produced by the sight of food, is skating on the thin ice of digestibility. When he begins to tax his poor digestive power by greedily gulping unmasticated rich food in large quantities and drinking ice water with it, he hardly realizes what he is doing.

Lack of hunger, catching cold—these innocent-looking troubles have a great deal to do with the happiness of man. The man newly choked by Mr. Cold bursts into germ-spreading, violent spells of sneezing. The sneezing bombards the fine cells of the mucous membrane, and the whole family of cells in the brain becomes disturbed. Due to the proximity of the brain and mental processes, the man with a cold feels miserable mentally.

By neglecting a cold in the head, a man allows it to spread its territory down to the throat. If he continues to neglect a cold, the wicked invader, Mr. Cold, enters the inner chambers of the bronchial tubes and tries to make a permanent settlement in his lungs.

Mr. Cold is known to be the "Happiness-Nagger." He may not be very dangerous on his first visit, but when he begins to visit you quite often, he can nag the happiness out of you.

ॐ ॐ ॐ

Curing a Cold

When you catch a cold, fast for two days. During a cold, the extra poisons in your body are being thrown off. If you eat food, you obstruct the poison-eliminating system of Nature with extra food chemicals.

If you cannot handle a complete fast, eat apples, pears, or grapes but refrain from eating acid fruits. Do not eat anything at night. Do not drink hot or cold water. Drink only two glasses of warm water daily. I believe that drinking too much water during a cold is not good because the extra water comes out constantly through the mucous membrane, making the nose run and causing irritation and accumulation of pus there. Fasting during a cold is very good for it helps Nature effect her own cure without interruption. At the beginning of a cold, it is very good to use a laxative suitable to your system.

A sunbath, with the rays of the sun falling directly on the epidermis of the body, has been known to cure a cold in one day. Protect sensitive skin by applying olive oil, or something similar, before taking a sunbath. A five- or ten-minute daily increase in sun bathing is a help for longer sun exposure. The best time for sunbaths is between 11 am and 3 pm.

ॐ ॐ ॐ

Eliminating Catarrh

Catarrh is caused mostly from overeating at night and from neglecting colds. By following these rules conscientiously, you will begin to destroy the roots of this disease.

If you are suffering from catarrh, make your evening meal very light: a fruit meal with ground nuts, or some cooked vegetables, perhaps boiled peas or spinach, just to satisfy the demands of your acquired habit. Refrain from eating meat as much as possible. Never eat fish, meat, or eggs at night. Drink milk in the afternoon. Eat your heaviest meal at noon. Eat very little bread, perhaps a small piece of toasted whole wheat bread at noon.

Do not drink water or eat right before going to bed. Sleep well covered, with windows opened wide both summer and winter. Take long walks in the morning, and especially at night before going to bed. Inhale and exhale deeply when walking.

ॐ ॐ ॐ

Exercise Until You Perspire

Don't complain of stomach troubles, colds, or headaches. These are always the outcome of a faulty diet or lack of physical exercise. Perform some sort of exercise every day until perspiration breaks out over your whole body. Your colds and other similar ills will soon disappear.

ॐ ॐ ॐ

A Morning Wash

A good internal morning wash: Add the juice of a fresh lime to a glassful of distilled water. Drink this upon rising, and then give the stomach a sort of churning exercise, visualizing a washing process taking place in the area of the navel.

ॐ ॐ ॐ

Alcohol Inhibits Soul Awareness

Alcohol benumbs the senses, deadens the reason, and inflames the baser passions and animal instincts. It is the enemy of reason, the great paralyzer of good judgment, and a destroyer of mankind.

Liquor corrodes the stomach and destroys intuition. It anaesthetizes the spiritual brain cells and eventually destroys permanently their ability to tune into God-consciousness. No instrument fine enough to perceive God can ever be devised—only the spiritual brain cells of man can do that. It is in your own best interest to avoid alcohol. Do that which will bring you lasting happiness.

ॐ ॐ ॐ

Fasting and Special Diets

Most diseases can be cured by judicious fasting—either partial or complete fasting—under the guidance of a specialist.

Partial fasting can include:

1. Limiting the diet to certain foods

2. Abstaining from certain foods

3. Limiting the food intake as to quantity

4. Limiting the number of meals to one or two per day.

Some of these forms of fasting may be combined. For example, to cure disease or reduce weight, a person may abstain from certain foods altogether and limit the intake of other foods.

More specific types of fasting are:

Liquid Diet: For one or two days a week, and whenever one does not feel hungry, confine the food intake to milk, orange juice, or any other fruit juice. Fasting one day a week on orange juice and taking a suitable laxative that day will help to keep the body cells firm and free from disease. A three-day fast once a month on orange juice, with a laxative each night while fasting, will expel poisons and do much to make the body strong, healthy, and youthful to the last days of life. Orange juice is very good because it counteracts the acids in the body caused by eating meats and heavy foods.

Solid Diet: This diet is confined to raw fruits, raw vegetables, and half-boiled vegetables, including the juice in which they were boiled. No sugar, bread or other starchy foods; no meat, eggs, or fish; nothing but the raw or lightly cooked fruits or vegetables, and only one meal per day—at noon. Drink plenty of water while on this diet.

The Nine-Day Diet*

The Nine-Day Cleansing and Vitalizing Diet has proven a most effective method for ridding the system of poisons. It consists of the following foods daily:

- 1 and 1/2 grapefruit
- 5 oranges
- 1 and 1/2 lemons
- 1 raw vegetable salad
- 1 cooked vegetable with juice (quantity optional)
- 3 cups Vitality Beverage (one at each meal)

* Be sure to check with a medical professional before doing this diet. This diet is not appropriate for people on blood thinners, or for those who are pregnant or who have diabetes.

- 1 glass orange juice with teaspoon of senna leaves or Original Swiss Kriss (To be taken every night during the cleansing diet, before going to bed. To obtain best results, take ½ teaspoon at first; later increase to 1 teaspoon.)

Vitality Beverage Ingredients
- 2 stalks chopped celery
- 2 cups chopped spinach, dandelion, or turnip greens
- 5 carrots (chopped) including part of stem
- 1 bunch chopped parsley
- 1 quart water
- No salt or spices

The beverage may be prepared in two ways, the first way being preferable:

1. After putting celery and carrots through a vegetable chopper, lightly boil them in water for ten minutes. Then add the leafy greens and parsley and boil ten minutes longer. Strain by squeezing through cheesecloth.

2. Use the same ingredients, but do not cook them. Put them through a vegetable juicer.

Drink one cup of the beverage at each of the three meals. This vitality beverage has been found to be a blood tonic and a very effective aid for rheumatism, various stomach disorders (including acute indigestion), chronic catarrh, bronchitis, and nervous strain.

While on the cleansing diet, strictly abstain from spices, candies, pastries, meat, eggs, fish, cheese, milk, butter, bread, fried foods, oil, beans—in fact, all foods not mentioned above.

If one feels the need of additional nourishment, take one tablespoonful of thoroughly ground nuts in half a glass of water or a glass of orange juice.

After the nine-day diet, you should be especially careful in the selection and quantity of your food for at least four days, and resume your normal diet gradually. Begin by adding a portion of cottage cheese to your meal. Almonds, egg yolk, and baked potato are among the first foods to be added. Do not overeat. Gradually increase the amount and variety until you are again on a normal diet.

If you are not successful in ridding the body of all poisons during the initial attempt, repeat the cleansing diet after two or three weeks.

Before going to bed every night while on the diet, it has been found beneficial to soak in two pounds of Epsom salts in one-fourth tub of warm water. It is also very helpful to take a salts bath every now and then for several weeks after finishing the cleansing diet.

❦ ❦ ❦

For Healthy Skin

A truly beautiful skin is a sign of internal cleanliness. The skin shares the burdens of the internal flushing system known as the urinary tract. When, through ignorance and neglect, we trespass the laws of physical equilibrium and build up excess toxins, the skin must help eliminate them.

About one fourth of the water taken into the body is eliminated, along with a large quantity of waste products, through the pores of the skin. To keep the skin functioning properly, wear light, loose clothing. Take a warm bath each night to wash off the accumulated waste of the day and to allow the skin to breathe at night. Take a cool or cold shower in the morning to keep the skin toned and to help it react properly as a heat regulator.

Add one quart of distilled water to a bunch of well washed parsley. Simmer until the leaves and stems are thoroughly withered. Let stand in a covered pot until cool. Strain. Drink several eight-ounce glasses a day for several days in succession. Parsley vibrates with the kidneys and flushes the organs of elimination.

❦ ❦ ❦

For a Beautiful Complexion

A lovely skin depends primarily on good health, and must be cultivated and maintained by purification from within. Pimples mean clogged pores; unsightly growths indicate excess carbohydrates in the diet (starches and sweets); wrinkles are Nature's hunger cries for vitalizing foods, iodine, and oil.

A dry skin wrinkles faster than one that is well lubricated, so outer aids are also helpful. Oil, particularly olive oil, has been used throughout the ages as an aid to skin beauty. Chief among Cleopatra's secrets of beauty and rejuvenation, so history tells us, was the generous use of olive oil. Secure a good brand of yellow olive oil. Use with strained lemon juice, half of each. The lemon prevents unseemly hair growth and assists the oil in penetrating. Almond oil is another excellent facial skin builder and a good base for powder.

Just as I frequently assure you that it is never too late to begin spiritual development, so I can say that it is never too late to begin a regime of skin rejuvenation. Remember that the countless cells of the skin, as well as of the body itself, undergo a constant process of birth, maturity, and decay. Like the snake, we can shed the old skin completely, though of course more gradually, and rebuild all-new skin tissue within a year.

The following foods may be classified as specific skin foods; use an abundance of them in salads and as vegetable cocktails: carrots, watercress, parsley, celery, cucumbers, and spinach.

ชี ชี ชี

For Skin Beauty

Do's

- Give your skin a daily air bath, as well as a sunbath.
- Apply lemon juice or fresh cucumber juice as a bleach to discolorations, then add a drop or two of olive oil.
- Take daily friction baths with a rough towel.
- Work up a good perspiration by some sort of exercise.
- Soothe, heal, and nourish skin with an oatmeal pack. It adds a unique aliveness and luster to the skin. Use steel cut oats, either as raw cereal mixed with water, or from leftover cooked cereal.

Do not's

- If the skin is too oily, it is often helpful, at least for some time, to discontinue the use of dairy products.

- Don't take too frequent or prolonged tub baths, unless for therapeutic purposes. While baths do relax, they also tend to dry the skin and to be demagnetizing to the body. The best time for hot baths is at night, unless in an emergency.
- Never wear tight elastic in clothing as this interferes with circulation.
- Never use the lard-based cold creams sold on the market. Many vegetable-based creams are now available. Or, prepare your own, using almond oil, olive oil and lemon, or other vegetable oils as a base.

ॐ ॐ ॐ

Smile for Health

There is no better reviving tonic than smiles. There is no better ornament than a genuine smile. There is no beauty greater than the smile of peace and wisdom glowing on your face.

ॐ ॐ ॐ

With blessings
Paramhansa Yogananda
Encinitas - April 3rd 1951

Chapter 6

The Art of Super-Relaxation

Super-Relaxation

People often talk of relaxation, but few know how to achieve it. Some people know how to relax physically but not mentally. Super-relaxation is complete, voluntary withdrawal of consciousness and energy from the entire body.

Complete mental relaxation consists in releasing the consciousness from the delusion of duality and resting the mind, identifying with one's own true nature of unity in Spirit. You have hypnotized yourselves into thinking that you are human beings, whereas in reality you are gods.

🐚 🐚 🐚

Rejuvenation through Relaxation

The mind must manifest calmness. Where the worries and trials of everyday life are concerned, the mind must be like water, which does not retain any impression of the waves that play on its bosom. That which can be attained unconsciously can also be attained consciously. Through the instructions on meditation *(below)*, one can achieve complete calmness in the heart, lungs, and other inner organs. When the muscles and inner organs are freed from motion by relaxation, the breaking down of bodily tissues and decay is temporarily inhibited. This helps to keep the bloodstream pure, for when there is decay going on in the body the waste products are thrown into the venous blood and poison it.

When tissues stop decaying, the venous blood ceases to accumulate in the body. This gives the heart a much needed rest; there is no longer a need for it to pump great quantities of venous blood into the lungs for purification, because the neutralized, electrified tissues do not require blood and oxygen. Thus, heart action and breathing become unnecessary. This leads to the release of enormous quantities of life current, which otherwise would be needed in the heart for the daily task of pumping tons of blood through the system. Thus, many billions of cells rest and depend on the sustaining life current to enable them to live in a conscious, undecaying state.

When the body cells learn the art of living without blood and oxygen, they truly know how to live by the life force coming in from the medulla.

When the energy is withdrawn from all the sensory nerves, the five sense-telephones are disconnected. No sensations can reach the brain and intelligence operators. The mind gains freedom from thoughts that begin in sensations, as well as the associated thoughts of subconscious memory. This leaves the scientifically freed mind unhampered to march Godward.

Enter into absolute silence every morning and banish thoughts for several minutes each time. Sit quietly and meditate on the joy of Silence. Think of that joy as communion with God. The more you meditate, the more you will realize that nothing else can give you that refined joy but the increasing joy of Silence. That joy-contact in meditation is contact with God. Pray deeply with devotion, first for God's love, then for wisdom, happiness, health, prosperity, and then for the fulfillment of any specific legitimate wish.

Physical Relaxation

For complete relaxation of the whole body, first gently tense the entire body. Then relax and withdraw all energy from the body and remain relaxed, without the slightest physical motion. The complete absence of motion and tension from muscles and limbs is "relaxation." Imagine that the body is jelly-like, without bones or muscles. When you can do this, you have attained perfect muscular relaxation.

Mental Relaxation

Mental relaxation signifies complete mental rest. You can achieve this by practicing going to sleep at will. Relax the body and think of the drowsiness you feel just before you fall asleep. Then try to reproduce that state. (Use imagination, not will, to do this.) Most people do not relax even while they sleep. Their minds are restless; hence they dream. Therefore, conscious mental relaxation is better than relaxation that is the by-product of passive physical relaxation, or sleep. In this way you can choose to dream or to keep dreams off your mental motion picture screen.

No matter how busy you are, do not forget now and then to free your mind completely from worries and all duties. Just dismiss them from your mind. Remember, you were not made for them; they were made *by* you. Do not allow them to torture you.

When you are beset by overwhelming mental trials or worries, try to fall asleep. If you can do that, you will find on awakening that mental tension is relieved and that worry has loosened its grip on you. Tell yourself that even if you died, the earth would continue to follow its orbit, and business would be carried on as usual; hence, why worry? When you take yourself too seriously, death comes to mock you and remind you of the brevity of material life and its duties.

Mental relaxation consists in the ability to free the attention at will from haunting worries over past and present difficulties; consciousness of constant duty; dread of accidents and other haunting fears; greed; passion; and disturbing thoughts and attachments. Mastery in mental relaxation comes with faithful practice. It can be attained by freeing the mind of all thoughts at will and keeping the attention fixed on the peace and contentment within. By regular practice of meditation you can divert the attention from worry to peace.

For this reason, the devotee who aspires to develop uniformly and steadily in spirituality must always keep the body quiet and not in perpetual motion and restlessness, keep the breath quiet by proper breathing exercises, preserve the vital essence by self-control and good company, and calm the mind with the practice of concentration and meditation.

You can learn to switch off the life current from the entire body through conscious will by the steady, conscientious practice of the Hong-Sau technique of concentration.

ॐ ॐ ॐ

The Hong-Sau Technique of Concentration

Breath is life. If you can live without breathing, you will prolong your life and rise above body-consciousness to soul-consciousness while still living in your physical body. To be truly breathless doesn't come about by suppressing the breath or holding it forcibly in the lungs. Rather, breathlessness lifts one to a state of inner calmness and relaxation, making it simply unnecessary for you to breathe for a time.

You can practice this technique at any time. Wherever you are, sit erect with your spine straight, and deeply relax. Close your eyes (or fix their gaze, eyes half closed, at the point between the eyebrows). Now, with deep calmness, mentally watch your breath, without controlling it, as it enters and exits the body. As the breath enters, move the index finger of your right hand inward, toward the thumb, and mentally (without moving your tongue or lips) chant "Hong." As the breath exits, straighten the index finger, and mentally chant "Sau" (pronounced "saw"). (The purpose for moving the index finger is to become more positive in your concentration, and to differentiate the inhalation from the exhalation.)

Do not in any way control the breath mentally. Assume, rather, the calm attitude of a silent observer, watching the breath's natural flow as it enters and exits the body—a flow of which you are generally not particularly aware.

Practice this technique with great reverence and attention for at least ten minutes (to begin with). The longer your practice, the better. You can practice it at any time, day or night, during formal meditation or in your leisure time—for instance, while riding in a car (provided you aren't driving!), or even while lying on your back in bed. It will give you a deep sense of inner calmness, and will bring you at last to the realization that you are not the body, but the soul—superior to and independent of this material body.

For formal meditation, sit on a straight-backed, armless chair. Place a woolen blanket over the chair, covering the back and letting it run down beneath your feet. Face east. Sit erect, away from the back of the chair.

The Hong-Sau technique can also be practiced, as I said, during leisure moments—such as sitting in a doctor's waiting room. Simply watch the breath, and as you do so, mentally chant "Hong" and "Sau," without moving the finger, closing the eyes, gazing upward at the point between the eyebrows, or doing anything that might attract the attention of others around you. Keep your eyes open, if you like, without blinking, perhaps looking straight ahead, or at some particular point. Keep the spine erect, if possible, and if you can do so unobtrusively.

The purpose of the Hong-Sau technique is to help you to free your attention from outwardness, and to withdraw it from the senses, for breath is the cord that keeps the soul tied to the body. Man lives in an atmosphere of air, which he requires even as a fish requires water. By rising above the breath in breathlessness, man can enter the celestial realms of light, where the angels dwell. By dispassionately watching

the breath coming in and going out, one's breathing naturally slows, calming at last the peace-disturbing activity of the
heart, lungs, and diaphragm.

Consider for a moment this extraordinary fact: The heart
normally pumps about twelve tons of blood a day! It gets
no rest even at night, when most of the other organs have a
chance to suspend their activity at least partially. The most
worked (and overworked) organ in the body is the heart.
The Hong-Sau technique is a scientific method for resting
the heart, increasing longevity thereby, and liberating a vast
amount of Life Current, or energy, to be distributed over
the whole body, renewing all the body cells and preventing
their decay.

This marvelous, though simple, technique is one of
India's greatest contributions to the world. It lengthens
man's lifespan, and is a practical method for rising above
body-consciousness and realizing oneself as the Immortal
Spirit. The words, Hong and Sau, are a Sanskrit saying, giv-
en mantric power. The original saying, "Aham saha," means,
"I—am He."

The Importance of Relaxation

In sleep, we experience sensory relaxation. Death is complete, though involuntary, relaxation of the spirit from the body. It comes after the arrest of the heart's action. By the Hong-Sau technique, one can reach the point of even relaxing the heart, and thereby rising above its compulsion to outwardness, experiencing death consciously, and eliminating one's sense of the mystery of death and the fear of dying. One can learn, indeed, to leave his body voluntarily and blissfully, instead of being thrown out of it forcefully, often as a complete surprise, at death.

Inattention during practice of this technique can be soporific, producing sleep. Concentrated attention, on the other hand, brings to every body cell a tingling sense of divine life.

If you have the time, practice the technique longer—indeed, as long as you like. I myself, as a boy, used to practice it for seven hours at a time, and thereby achieved a deep state of breathless trance. Hold to the great calmness you feel during and after this practice. Cling to that peace as long as possible. Apply it in practical life situations, when dealing with people, when studying, when doing business, when thinking. And use it to help you to practice self-control, when trying to rid yourself of some deep-seated, harmful mental or emotional habit. Whenever a situation demands it, recall to mind the calmness you've felt during and after the practice of this technique, and, reliving that state, meet the situation from that calm inner center, where your natural soul-intuition will ensure the best possible outcome.

Remember, deep intensity of concentration is necessary for the correct practice of this technique. This does not mean, however, that there should be any sense of strain present. Practice the technique calmly, with relaxation—even with reverence—and feel in that calmness that you are placing yourself in readiness to listen to, and to become absorbed in, the Cosmic Vibration, AUM. Hong-Sau will help to put you in contact with the Great Spirit, who is present in you as your soul, and whose expression is vibration, the cause of that inner sound. Results will positively come, and deep calmness will be yours. Higher intuitions will come to you after prolonged practice, and you will find yourself in touch with the unexplored reservoir of divine power.

Do not be impatient. Keep on steadily. Incorporate this practice into your regular routine, making it as much a part of your day as eating, brushing your teeth and bathing, or sleeping. Supremely beneficial effects will pervade your whole mental and physical constitution.

As in everything else, the highest results cannot be attained in a day or even in days. Practice! Practice the technique, and apply to your daily needs the calmness it produces. Remember also that I speak from experience—not only my own, but that of centuries of experience by the great yogis in my country. You, too, can have the same glorious experience as they, if you persevere in your practice.

Final Important Point: Where to Concentrate?

Where should you focus your attention, while practicing this technique? On the breath, yes, but where in the body?

Your attention, at first, may be on the pumping lungs and diaphragm. Concentrate first, then, on that physical movement. Gradually, as the mind grows calm, shift your attention from the body to the breath itself. Be aware of the breath where it enters the body, in the nostrils. As you grow calmer still, try to feel where, in the nostrils, the flow is strongest. At first it will be at the outer nostrils themselves, but as your concentration deepens try to feel the breath higher in the nose, and note where the flow seems strongest. Is it in the upper part of the nose? the sides? the bottom? This can even help you to perceive more clearly your own state of mind. In the upper part, the flow may indicate a higher awareness. In the lower, a certain downward flow of energy in the spine. On the outer sides of the nostrils, the flow may reflect a tendency somewhat to react emotionally. Toward the center of the nostrils, there may be a tendency toward withdrawal. As you grow still calmer, feel the breath where it enters the head, up by the point between the eyebrows—the actual seat of concentration in the body.

The origin of the breath lies in the astral body. Astral inhalation corresponds to an upward movement through what is known in the Yoga teachings as *iḍa*. Astral exhalation corresponds to a downward movement through the *pingala* nerve channel. These channels may be observed by those who eat fish as the two little nerves that run down the length of the spine.

An upward flow of energy through *iḍa* accompanies inhalation of the physical breath. And a downward flow through *pingala* accompanies physical exhalation. Astral breathing is accomplished by this upward and downward movement of energy. It is intrinsic to the reactive process. When the upward flow of energy is stronger, a positive reaction is indicated, and the same is true with deliberate physical inhalation. When the movement is more strongly downward (or when the physical exhalation is stronger than the inhalation), it comes out as a sigh, and indicates a feeling of rejection. When the inhalation is longer than the exhalation, it is an indication of positive reaction—even one of excitement. When the exhalation is longer, there is a corresponding withdrawal into oneself. In sleep, the exhalation is twice as long as the inhalation. When inhalation and exhalation are equal in duration, there is inner equanimity.

ॐ ॐ ॐ

Another Technique for Relaxation

First, close your eyes and expel the breath; switch off the attention and energy from the senses. Feel and mentally watch the heart and circulation. Calm the heart by the command of will, as you stop a watch by gently touching its spring. With calmness you can arrest the activities of the entire physical machinery. Then switch on the Life Current in the spine and brain, disconnecting your Life Current from the five sense telephones. Convert your brain into a divine radio, receiving the Cosmic Sound of AUM.

ॐ ॐ ॐ

Super-relaxation with AUM

Sit on a straight chair, with your spine upright. Expel the breath quickly, and keep the breath out, counting mentally 1 to 10. Inhale slowly, hold breath, counting 1 to 10. Repeat ten times. Then expel the breath and forget it.

Concentrate on the toes of the left foot and say "AUM" mentally on each toe. Do the same to the toes of the right foot. Then concentrate on the sole of the left foot and then the right foot, saying, "AUM" on each. Concentrate on the left and right calves, mentally saying "AUM." Do the same with the left and right thighs, left and right hips, navel, abdomen, liver, spleen, stomach, pancreas, heart, left and right lungs, left and right hands and arms, left side of neck, right side of neck, front and back of neck.

Say "AUM" mentally, concentrating on the pituitary gland, pineal gland, medulla, point between the eyebrows, mouth, tongue and uvula, left and right nostrils, left and right eyes, left and right ears, cerebellum, and cerebrum. Then go up and down the chakras: coccygeal, sacral, lumbar, dorsal, cervical, medulla, and Christ Center at the point between the eyebrows, mentally chanting "AUM." Try to feel that the whole body is surrounded within and without with the holy vibration of "AUM."

ॐ ॐ ॐ

Omnipresence

O Spirit, release my life and consciousness from possessions, from attachments. Release, Thou, my life and mind from the tensed body. Release my consciousness from the senses, and then from the breath. Unlock the energy from the heart.

Then, O Spirit, lodge life and consciousness in the spine. And then release them unto the Spirit into Infinite Spaces. O, let me behold Milky Way Spiral Nebulae floating and glimmering in me.

Bring the bright Bird of Omnipresence back through its cage door of the medulla into the passage of the spine, and let it fly into the heart and sing vitality there. Let it flutter its wings of breaths into the two lungs. Then, O Spirit, let it flutter at last over the walls of flesh.

AUM...vibrate in the hands, in the feet, in the body, in the muscles! AUM...vibrate in the Spirit! AUM...come back to the spine, back to the heart, and back to the muscles again!

🕉 🕉 🕉

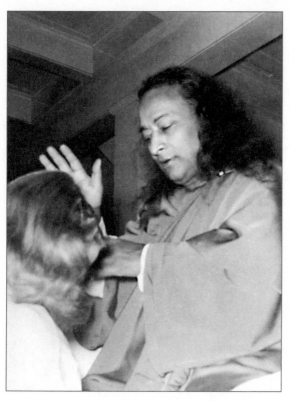

Chapter 7

God's Healing Power

You Are Immortal

Resurrect your soul from the dreams of frailties. Resurrect your soul in eternal wisdom. What is the method? Relaxation! Self-control. Right diet. Right fortitude. Undaunted attitude of the mind. Refuse to be defeated. Don't acknowledge defeat. To acknowledge defeat is greater defeat. You have unlimited power — you must cultivate that power, that is all.

Meditation is the greatest way of resurrecting your soul from the bondage of body and all your trials. Meditation! Meditate at the feet of the Infinite. Learn to saturate yourself with Him. Your trials may be great, but the greatest enemy of yourself is yourself! You are immortal, your trials are mortal. They are changeable, you are unchangeable. You can unleash the eternal powers and shatter your trials.

ॐ ॐ ॐ

The Healing Power of Faith

No disease is incurable. Some diseases are beyond the reach of medicines, which by their nature are limited. When a disease is persistent and long lasting, and medical aid and other ordinary methods fail to cure it, it is then called chronic or incurable.

The deficiency in the medicine and its inability to cure are illogically transferred to the disease. The medicine is uncurative—so doctors call the disease incurable! But the power of the Infinite is unlimited and can heal all disease.

Medicine has its uses—why deny facts?—but it is confined to certain limits. If a disease is beyond medical aid, that is not the time to despair but rather the time to put your faith in the Infinite Power, who is omnipotent.

Medicine cannot help you if you just talk about it and do not use it; similarly, faith cannot cure unless you use it, and not simply talk about it.

In mental or spiritual healing, one must have faith to "burn the boat and walk on the sea." Shouldn't you doubt the aid of limited material forces rather than the power of the Infinite Spirit?

ॐ ॐ ॐ

Healing through Vibrations

God wants His children to enjoy health and happiness, but they create disease and sorrow by breaking His laws.

God is harmony, and when man, made in His image, tries to lead an inharmonious life, he hurts himself. God never punishes man. Man punishes himself by reaping the results of his self-created wrong actions.

There are diseases that result from breaking hygienic laws and the consequent bacterial invasion. There are maladies that result from disobeying the mental laws of Being and the consequent attack of mental bacteria of fear, anger, worry, greed, temptation, and lack of self-control. There are diseases that arise from the soul's ignorance.

Remember that ignorance is the mother of all physical, mental, and spiritual diseases. Abolish ignorance by contacting God, and body, mind, and soul will be healed of all maladies.

Human life can be likened to a house fitted with three windows of the body, mind, and soul. Through these openings come pouring forth the three different kinds of perfect light of God—known as health rays, faculty rays, and wisdom rays. These triune rays are responsible for the perfect health, mental equanimity, and enlightenment of the soul of man. That is why man is spoken of as being created in the image of God. But if man is made in God's likeness, why does he suffer in so many ways? The answer is: Man as a divine child has independence.

Man was made as a god, and as such he has the privilege and free choice of the great God to eclipse that image with error, or to keep it unobscured and dazzling with rays of health, power, and peace. Man has the peculiar independence and free will to live in the house of life with its health-, strength-, and light-giving windows open or closed. When he closes the windows of life, the conscious Cosmic Rays are shut out and man lives in the darkness of physical disease, mental disquietude, or abysmal soul-ignorance.

Most people have had one or more of their windows of life jammed shut for years. That is why they suffer from chronic maladies. Their rescue lies in discovering how to open their windows themselves and bask once more in the all-healing conscious Cosmic Rays.

Man wants instantaneous healing by God's power, but he fails to understand that the work of healing lies with himself, and that God never wanted him to be sick in the first place. God gave man the original privilege and free choice to receive rays or to shut them out. God cannot change his law arbitrarily just by the bribery of special ceremonies, blind prayer, or partiality. He can be moved only by the law and by love. Love is law. When man has closed the health-power-and-light-giving windows of life and has kept them closed indefinitely, he must himself make the effort to open those windows again and let the freely-willing-to-help, knocking-to-enter Light in.

All physical diseases, psychological inharmonies, and soul maladies born of ignorance come from man's own mistake of shutting out the rays of God. Whether man knowingly or unknowingly shut the health-giving windows of life, the logical conclusion is that now he must open them again by self-effort. Ignorance of the law will not save him from the effects of a law that was broken.

There are many ways of opening the three jammed windows of life. Those ways are generally called healing. Healing can be classified as physical healing; psychological healing of worries, fears, nervousness, etc.; and spiritual healing of soul-ignorance.

There are many types of healing, each of which can be used in healing physical, mental, or spiritual diseases. Of the different kinds of healing—such as medicine, injection, affirmation, massage, nerve or vertebrae adjustment, imagination, will, or faith—vibratory healing is of great importance.

Vibratory healing for oneself consists in experiencing willpower-charged energy internally, or in using superconscious chanting, intonations of the human voice, enlivening words, phrases, and affirmations.

The methods of internal vibrations of energy can only be used by following a system of spiritual exercises such as Yogoda offers. Willingness and determination keep the blood vitalized with life-energy. If you can keep this mental initiative and willing-to-work attitude all the time, you will find your blood charged with life-current, making it immune to the invasion of bacteria. Keeping yourself smiling from within, pulsating with joy, ever ready to serve, and spiritually ambitious in helping others—all these keep the body constantly supplied with fresh Cosmic Energy drawn into the body through the door of the medulla oblongata. Strong will draws energy from the conscious Cosmic Rays surrounding the body.

Therefore, strengthen your will and determination in everything. Your body will then be internally vibrating with life current. A man of strong will, by his highly vibrating mind, can shake out disease, failure, and ignorance, but the will vibration must be stronger than the vibration of disease. The more chronic the disease, the stronger, steadier, and more unflinching should be the determination, faith, and effort of the will to get well.

Chanting

In connection with singing, chanting, or intoning away physical disease, worry, or spiritual ignorance, one must know the law of intonation: from loud to quiet, quiet to whisper, whisper to mental, and subconscious to superconscious. This is the method of converting meaningful words into realized experiences—assimilating the truth until it becomes part of the soul's realization. Or one must induce the superconscious, peaceful state first and from that stage chant mentally, quietly, or loudly, as he pleases.

The words, whether said aloud or mentally only, must be injected with superconscious faith and steadiness to accomplish a specific healing. Mental chanting is best for individuals; loud chanting, ranging from low to high, or vice versa, is good in congregations.

Before chanting, the law of repetition should be understood. Western minds often fail to grasp the changing depths of conviction in Hindu chanting and see only a monotonous repetition of a word or words. Of course, repetition of words without experiencing their meaning with deep and deeper feelings and realization is useless. That is what the Bible meant by, "Take not the name of the Lord thy God in vain": that is, do not say, "O, God, O, God" without attention, or while the mind is wandering. Long intellectual prayers full of word-jugglery, but without soul, are only empty noises.

It is better to say just one phrase, such as "O, Father, heal me," or "I am well, for Thou art in me," extemporaneously repeating it vigorously from loud voice to whisper, and lastly from a whisper to mental affirmation, until one feels what one is saying—that is, repeating a phrase with increasing depth of soul-feeling until one realizes the meaning of his utterance in every fiber of his being.

The moment the phrase reaches the superconscious and the inner conviction, a volley of energy will shoot down and heal the body, mind, and soul, electrocuting physical bacteria, paralyzing mental fears, and conflagrating ignorance into ashes.

The police commissioner of Chicago recently declared that if the sounds of vehicles could be cut down, city people would live ten years longer. In other words, inharmonious noise affects the nervous system of people, weakening the medium through which vital energy is supplied to all the principal organs of the body. With the deterioration of the nervous system, the energy and blood supply become low, making the body a fit home for disease.

On the other hand, harmonious sounds and chants impregnated with superconscious soul force, will power, and faith, awaken the drooping tissues of the nervous system by rousing vital energy in them. In this way, voice vibrations can heal all inharmonious conditions of the body, mind, and soul. A sincere, kind word, an inspired song, and a soul-solacing voice of wisdom have dispelled many sorrows and inflamed many with the light of lasting joy.

❦ ❦ ❦

A Saint Is Healed

A certain man was dying of diabetes. The doctors had given him three months to live. He determined, in the time remaining to him, to find God. He sat in meditation, gradually extending to longer and longer periods the time he could sit. At first, it was only fifteen minutes at a time, after which he needed to get up and relieve himself. Slowly, however, he sat longer until finally he was meditating several hours at a stretch. Constantly he prayed, "Lord, come into my broken temple!"

The allotted three months passed. Still he lived, and was sitting for steadily longer periods. Three years passed: still he was alive. At last one day God appeared to him. The man, emerging from his ecstasy, discovered that his body was completely healed.

"Lord," he cried, "I didn't ask You to heal me. All I asked was that You come into my broken temple." And the Lord answered, "Where My light is, there no darkness can come. The saint—for he'd become one—then wrote in the sand, "And on this day the Lord came into my broken temple, and made it whole!"

What will power! If you tried that hard, how fast you would go! You all have strong will power. I urge you, Use it!

ॐ ॐ ॐ

God's Power Is Unlimited

All diseases are the result of collisions of a brittle inharmonious life with the stone wall of God's harmony within. Peaceful actions attune with God's peace as felt in silence within, and the result is happiness. Wrong actions collide with God's peace of silence and produce unhappiness and ill health.

No doubt some medicines have healing power, since God gave herbs and minerals the power to affect the body of man, but medicines and doctors have only limited power and often reveal their helplessness in cases of chronic disease.

What destroys pain and ignorance and prevents accidents forever, so that your body, mind, and soul will be the perfect image of Spirit? It is this: Convince your mind that all human methods of cure are limited in their healing power, and that only God's all-permeating, all-healing power is unlimited.

Remember, a beggar gets only a beggar's share, but a son receives a son's share. Do not beg for money or health. Rather, demand your lost divine birthright of oneness with the Father. When that is accomplished by the ever-increasing, ever-new joy contact of God in silence, then all things, including health, abundance, and wisdom, will be added unto you. The soul, mind, and body will be perceived as the perfect manifestation of God Himself. It is after such realization that the body can remain permanently healed.

Finally, man should depend more and more on the limitless inner source of Cosmic Consciousness and less and less on the other sources of body energy. The highest form of rejuvenation is to unite the human consciousness and Cosmic Consciousness through meditation.

By constantly holding the peaceful after-effects of meditation in mind, by feeling immortality in the body, by believing in eternal life instead of the illusory changes of life, and by feeling the ocean of immortal Bliss God underlying all experiences, the soul can find not only perpetual rejuvenation in the soul, but also in the body. As soon as the body is found to be not isolated from Spirit but vibrating currents in the ocean of Cosmic Consciousness, then the perpetual rejuvenation of the Spirit can be implanted in the body.

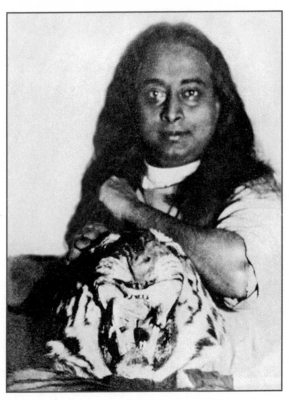

Appendix

Valuable Yogoda Exercises from Yogananda's Original Lessons

Valuable Yogoda Exercises from Yogananda's Original Lessons

1.   Stand erect with arms stretched straight above your head. Relax while holding this position. Throw the breath out and keep breath out, counting 1 to 12. Inhale and feel that you are drawing in energy through the fingertips into the medulla and body parts.

2.   Stretch arms out to the sides parallel to the floor. Exhale and bring palms together, relaxing all body parts. Then inhale, tensing body parts 1 to 20, as you stretch arms backward out to the sides. Relax, exhaling slowly, bringing palms together. Repeat twice.

3.   Lengthwise tension: Tense (low, medium, high) left calf and relax, then left thigh and relax. Right calf and then right thigh; left forearm, left upper arm; right forearm, right upper arm. Repeat each part three times.

4.   Close eyes. Very gently contract both breasts. Put the whole attention there while contracting them. Hold contraction, counting 1 to 30. Then release contraction. Repeat six times, morning, noon, and night.

5.   Lower chin to chest, tightening muscles of the throat. Slowly inhale, lifting head up and bending it backward. Relax, drop chin on chest, and exhale.

6. Medulla memory exercise: Relax head forward so that chin touches chest. Touch the first three fingertips of each hand together, and then press these six fingers on the medulla. Give a circular massage from left to right, five times. Keep the fingers well pressed on the medulla as you lift head and stretch it backward as far as possible toward the spine, tensing the back of neck. Relax. Then quickly drop head toward the chest, still keeping fingers in position, and repeat twice more.

7. Tense the whole left arm (fore and upper arm). Vibrate. Keep elbow at side. Lift forearm to shoulder as if lifting a weight of 5 to 25 pounds. Relax (withdraw energy) and drop. Repeat exercise with right arm and then both arms together.

8. Stretch arms out to the sides parallel to the floor with palms upward. Tense both arms and vibrate. Bend them at elbows slowly as if pulling a heavy weight from each side. Relax; drop arms to side. Repeat twice.

9. Plant feet firmly on ground. Lift straight arms out to the side, parallel to the floor. Then swing body and arms, so that the left arm goes behind you and the right palm hits the center of the chest; then swing the right arm behind and the left palm hits the center of the chest. Repeat five times. This exercise helps the spine and brain.

10. Stomach Exercises: These stomach exercises will help peristaltic movement and digestion, eliminating constipation and reducing obesity. To be practiced daily in the morning after arising.

A. Stoop forward grasping the arms of a chair, keeping your own arms straight. Exhale quickly and completely, and close nostrils and mouth with the fingers of left hand. With breath expelled, slowly draw in abdomen as far as possible, then push it out as far as possible. Continuing to hold breath expelled, repeat twice. Inhale. Repeat the above entire exercise five times. If you have stomach trouble, repeat ten times.

B. Stand erect with closed eyes. Press both hands on abdomen one above the other. Contract and tense to high tension the lower portion of abdomen. Hold that tension and contract and tense the upper abdomen. Relax both. Repeat six times.

11. Imaginary Rope Jumping Exercise: Swing your hands as if you are swinging a rope and jump over the imaginary rope.

12. Indoor walking or running: Stand four feet away from an open window in your room, or on an open porch. Take off your shoes and, standing in one place, go through

the motions of walking or running. First, hit the heel of the left foot against the left hip and bend right arm up, elbow remaining by your side, then drop left foot to the ground and your right arm to your side. Then raise the right foot, hitting the heel of the right foot against the right hip and bending left arm up, keeping elbow at side. Then go on alternating left and right until you feel that you have done enough, or until you perspire without much discomfort. If you count, walk or run from 25 to 400 steps.

If you do the indoor walking and running exercises twice daily in fresh air, it will do much to keep your body fit. When tired, practice the walking and running exercises several times, as well as the tensing and relaxing exercises, until fatigue leaves you. (People who have weak hearts should not practice the running exercise.)

Index

About the Author

Paramhansa Yogananda

"As a bright light shining in the midst of darkness, so was Yogananda's presence in this world. Such a great soul comes on earth only rarely, when there is a real need among men."

—The Shankaracharya of Kanchipuram

Born in India in 1893, Paramhansa Yogananda was trained from his early years to bring India's ancient science of Self-realization to the West. In 1920 he moved to the United States to begin what was to develop into a worldwide work touching millions of lives. Americans were hungry for India's spiritual teachings, and for the liberating techniques of yoga.

In 1946 he published what has become a spiritual classic and one of the best-loved books of the twentieth century, *Autobiography of a Yogi.* In addition, Yogananda established headquarters for a worldwide work, wrote a number of books and study courses, gave lectures to thousands in most major cities across the United States, wrote music and poetry, and trained disciples. He was invited to the White House by Calvin Coolidge, and he initiated Mahatma Gandhi into Kriya Yoga, his most advanced meditation technique.

Yogananda's message to the West highlighted the unity of all religions, and the importance of love for God combined with scientific techniques of meditation.

Further Explorations

If you are inspired by this book and would like to learn more about Yogananda's teachings, we offer many additional resources:

*Crystal Clarity publishes the original 1946, unedited edition of
Paramhansa Yogananda's spiritual masterpiece*

AUTOBIOGRAPHY OF A YOGI
Paramhansa Yogananda

One of the best-selling Eastern philosophy titles of all time, with millions of copies sold, this book was named one of the best and most influential books of the twentieth century. This highly prized reprinting of the original 1946 edition is the only one available free from textual changes made after Yogananda's death.

In this updated edition are bonus materials, including a last chapter that Yogananda wrote in 1951, without posthumous changes, the eulogy that Yogananda wrote for Gandhi, and a new foreword and afterword by Swami Kriyananda, one of Yogananda's close, direct disciples.

PRAISE FOR AUTOBIOGRAPHY OF A YOGI

"In the original edition, published during Yogananda's life, one is more in contact with Yogananda himself." —*David Frawley, Director, American Institute of Vedic Studies, author of* Yoga and Ayurveda

ALSO AVAILABLE AS AN **UNABRIDGED AUDIOBOOK IN MP3 FORMAT**

*Crystal Clarity is also pleased to offer these two biographies
of Paramhansa Yogananda by his direct disciple, Swami Kriyananda.*

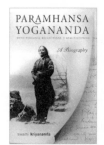

PARAMHANSA YOGANANDA

A BIOGRAPHY WITH PERSONAL REFLECTIONS
AND REMINISCENCES
Swami Kriyananda

Taking up where Yogananda's celebrated *Auto-biography of a Yogi* leaves off., this book will thrill the millions of readers of Yogananda's autobiography with scores of new stories from Yogananda's life—some charmingly human, some deeply inspiring, and many recounting miracles equal to those of the Bible. These stories are told from first-hand experience, and bring the Master alive unlike any other book ever written about him.

Now, Swami Kriyananda brilliantly puts to rest many misconceptions about his great guru, and reveals Yogananda's many-sided greatness. The author's profound grasp of the purpose of Yogananda's life, his inner nature, and his plans for the future are revelatory and sublime. Included is an insider's portrait of the great teacher's last years. More than a factual biography, this book also outlines the great master's key teachings.

Feel the power of Paramhansa Yogananda's divine consciousness and his impact on the world as presented with clarity and love by one of his few remaining direct disciples.

THE NEW PATH
MY LIFE WITH PARAMHANSA YOGANANDA
Swami Kriyananda

This is the moving story of Kriyananda's years
with Paramhansa Yogananda, India's emissary to
the West and the first yoga master to spend the
greater part of his life in America.

When Swami Kriyananda discovered *Autobio-
graphy of a Yogi* in 1948, he was totally new to Eastern teachings.
This is a great advantage to the Western reader, since Kriyananda
walks us along the yogic path as he discovers it from the moment of
his initiation as a disciple of Yogananda. With winning honesty, hu-
mor, and deep insight, he shares his journey along the spiritual path
through personal stories and experiences.

PRAISE FOR THE NEW PATH

"Reading *Autobiography of a Yogi* by Yogananda was a transformative
experience for me and for millions of others. In *The New Path* . . . Swami
Kriyananda carries on this great tradition. Highly recommended." —*Dean
Ornish, MD, Founder and President, Preventative Medicine Research Institute, Clinical
Professor of Medicine, University of California, San Francisco, author of* The Spectrum

"Required reading for every spiritual seeker. I heartily recommend it."
—*Michael Toms, Founder, New Dimensions Media, and author of* An Open Life:
Joseph Campbell in Conversation with Michael Toms

ALSO AVAILABLE AS AN **UNABRIDGED AUDIOBOOK IN MP3 FORMAT**

Crystal Clarity is also pleased to offer an important series of scriptural interpretations based on the teachings of Paramhansa Yogananda.

REVELATIONS OF CHRIST
PROCLAIMED BY PARAMHANSA YOGANANDA,
Presented by His Disciple, Swami Kriyananda

Over the past years, our faith has been severely shaken by experiences such as the breakdown of church authority, discoveries of ancient texts that supposedly contradict long-held beliefs, and the sometimes outlandish historical analyses of Scripture by academics. Together, these forces have helped create confusion and uncertainty about the true teachings and meanings of Christ's life.

This soul-stirring book, presenting the teachings of Christ from the experience and perspective of Yogananda, finally offers the fresh understanding of Christ's teachings for which the world has been waiting, in a more reliable way than any other: by learning from those saints who have communed directly, in deep ecstasy, with Christ and God.

PRAISE FOR REVELATIONS OF CHRIST

"This is a great gift to humanity. It is a spiritual treasure to cherish and to pass on to children for generations. This remarkable and magnificent book brings us to the doorway of a deeper, richer embracing of Eternal Truth." —*Neale Donald Walsch, author of* Conversations with God

ALSO AVAILABLE AS AN UNABRIDGED AUDIOBOOK IN MP3 FORMAT

THE ESSENCE OF THE BHAGAVAD GITA
EXPLAINED BY PARAMHANSA YOGANANDA
As Remembered by His Disciple, Swami Kriyananda

Rarely in a lifetime does a new spiritual classic appear that has the power to change people's lives and transform future generations. This is such a book.

This revelation of India's best-loved scripture approaches it from a fresh perspective, showing its deep allegorical meaning and its down-to-earth practicality. The themes presented are universal: how to achieve victory in life in union with the divine; how to prepare for life's "final exam," death, and what happens afterward; and, how to triumph over all pain and suffering.

PRAISE FOR THE ESSENCE OF THE BHAGAVAD GITA

"A brilliant text that will greatly enhance the spiritual life of every reader."
—*Caroline Myss, author of* Anatomy of the Spirit *and* Sacred Contracts

"It is doubtful that there has been a more important spiritual writing in the last fifty years than this soul-stirring, monumental work. What a gift! What a treasure!" —*Neale Donald Walsch, author of* Conversations with God

"I loved reading this!" —*Fred Alan Wolf, Ph.D., physicist, aka Dr. Quantum, author of* Dr. Quantum's Little Book of Big Ideas *and* The Yoga of Time Travel

"It has the power to change your life." —*Bernie Siegel, MD, author of* 101 Exercises for the Soul *and* Love, Medicine and Miraclesl

ALSO AVAILABLE AS AN **UNABRIDGED AUDIOBOOK IN MP3 FORMAT**
AND AS **PAPERBACK WITHOUT COMMENTARY**: THE BHAGAVAD GITA

WHISPERS FROM ETERNITY
Paramhansa Yogananda
Edited by His Disciple, Swami Kriyananda

Yogananda was not only a spiritual master, but a master poet, whose poems revealed the hidden divine presence behind even everyday things.

Open this book, pick a poem at random, and read it. Mentally repeat whatever phrase appeals to you. Within a short time, you will feel your consciousness transformed. This book has the power to rapidly accelerate your spiritual growth, and provides hundreds of delightful ways for you to begin your own conversation with God.

ALSO AVAILABLE AS AN **UNABRIDGED AUDIOBOOK IN MP3 FORMAT**

ENERGIZATION EXERCISES
Paramhansa Yogananda, Swami Kriyananda. and others

The *Energization Exercises*, as taught in the Ananda Course in Self-Realization, are a wonderful system of exercises originated by Paramhansa Yogananda. Best learned at Ananda, they are also taught here in a variety of formats.

Based on ancient teachings and eternal realities, Yogananda explains that the whole physical universe, including man, is surrounded by, and made of cosmic energy. Through daily use of these exercises we can systematically recharge our bodies with greater energy and train our minds to understand the true source of that power.

AVAILABLE IN **DVD, BOOKLET, BOOK. AND INSTRUCTIONAL CD**

THE WISDOM OF YOGANANDA SERIES

This series features writings of Paramhansa Yogananda not available elsewhere. Included are writings from his earliest years in America, in an approachable, easy-to-read format and presented with minimal editing, to capture his expansive and compassionate wisdom, his sense of fun, and his practical spiritual guidance.

HOW TO BE HAPPY ALL THE TIME
THE WISDOM OF YOGANANDA SERIES, VOLUME 1
Paramhansa Yogananda

Yogananda powerfully explains everything needed to lead a happier, more fulfilling life. Topics include: looking for happiness in the right places; choosing to be happy; tools and techniques for achieving happiness; sharing happiness with others; and balancing success and happiness.

"A fine starting point for reaching contentment." — *Bookwatch*

KARMA AND REINCARNATION
THE WISDOM OF YOGANANDA SERIES, VOLUME 2
Paramhansa Yogananda

Yogananda reveals the truth behind karma, death, reincarnation, and the afterlife. With clarity and simplicity, he makes the mysterious understandable. Topics include: why we see a world of suffering and inequality; how to handle the challenges in our lives; what happens at death, and after death; and the origin and purpose of reincarnation.

SPIRITUAL RELATIONSHIPS
THE WISDOM OF YOGANANDA SERIES, VOLUME 3
Paramhansa Yogananda

This book contains practical guidance and fresh insight on relationships of all types. Topics include: how to cure bad habits that can end true friendship; how to choose the right partner and create a lasting marriage; sex in marriage and how to conceive a spiritual child; problems that arise in marriage and what to do about them; the Universal Love behind all your relationships, and many more.

"[A] thoroughly 'user friendly' guide on how yoga principles can actually help relationships grow and thrive. Yogananda's keys to understanding yoga's underlying philosophy [teach] how to cure bad habits, expand love boundaries, and understand relationship problems."

—*James A. Cox, Chief Editor,* The Bookwatch

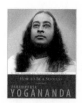

HOW TO BE A SUCCESS
THE WISDOM OF YOGANANDA SERIES, VOLUME 4
Paramhansa Yogananda

This book includes the complete text of *The Attributes of Success*, the original booklet later published as *The Law of Success*. In addition, you will learn how to find your purpose in life, develop habits of success and eradicate habits of failure, develop your will power and magnetism, and thrive in the right job.

Winner of the 2011 International Book Award for the Best Self-Help Book of the Year

HOW TO HAVE COURAGE, CALMNESS AND CONFIDENCE
THE WISDOM OF YOGANANDA SERIES, VOLUME 5
Paramhansa Yogananda

Everyone can be courageous, calm, and confident, because these are qualities of the soul. Hypnotized with material thinking and desires, many of us have lost touch with our inner power. In this potent book of spiritual wisdom, Paramhansa Yogananda shares the most effective steps for reconnecting with your divine nature.

"Make space on your desk for this little book. Pick it up often, read it, practice what it teaches, and watch happiness flow into your life." —*Krysta Gibson, editor of* New Spirit Journal

THE ESSENCE OF SELF-REALIZATION
THE WISDOM OF PARAMHANSA YOGANANDA
Recorded, Compiled, & Edited by His Disciple,
* Swami Kriyananda*

With nearly three hundred sayings rich with spiritual wisdom, this book is the fruit of a labor of love. A glance at the table of contents will convince the reader of the vast scope of this book. It offers as complete an explanation of life's true purpose, and of the way to achieve that purpose, as may be found anywhere.

MEDITATION FOR STARTERS

Swami Kriyananda

Have you wanted to learn to meditate, but just never got around to it? Or tried "sitting in the silence" only to find yourself too restless to stay more than a few moments? If so, *Meditation for Starters* is just what you've been looking for, and with a companion CD, it provides everything you need to begin a meditation practice. It is filled with easy-to-follow instructions, beautiful guided visualizations, and answers to important questions on meditation, such as: what meditation is (and isn't); how to relax your body and prepare yourself for going within; and techniques for interiorizing and focusing the mind.

CONVERSATIONS WITH YOGANANDA

Edited with commentary by Swami Kriyananda

This is an unparalleled, first-hand account of the teachings of Paramhansa Yogananda. Featuring nearly 500 never-before-released stories, sayings, and insights, this is an extensive, yet eminently accessible, fund of wisdom from one of the twentieth century's most famous yoga masters. Compiled and edited with commentary by Swami Kriyananda, one of Yogananda's closest direct disciples.

"This book is a treasure trove. If your goal is to grow spiritually, get a copy now." —*Richard Salva, author of* Walking with William of Normandy: A Paramhansa Yogananda Pilgrimage Guide

MUSIC AND AUDIOBOOKS

We offer many of our book titles in unabridged MP3 format audiobooks. To purchase these titles and to see more music and audiobook offerings, visit our website: www.crystalclarity.com. Or look for us in the popular online download sites.

METAPHYSICAL MEDITATIONS
Swami Kriyananda

Kriyananda's soothing voice guides you in thirteen different meditations based on the soul-inspiring, mystical poetry of Yogananda. Each meditation is accompanied by beautiful classical music to help you quiet your thoughts and prepare for deep states of meditation. Includes a full recitation of Yogananda's poem "Samadhi." A great aid to the serious meditator, as well as to those just beginning their practice.

RELAX: MEDITATIONS FOR FLUTE AND CELLO
Donald Walters
Featuring David Eby and Sharon Nani

This CD is specifically designed to slow respiration and heart rate, bringing listeners to their calm center. This recording features fifteen melodies for flute and cello, accompanied by harp, guitar, keyboard, and strings. Excellent for creating a calming atmosphere for work and home.

AUM: MANTRA OF ETERNITY
Swami Kriyananda

This recording features nearly seventy minutes of continuous vocal chanting of AUM, the Sanskrit word meaning peace and oneness of spirit, as extensively discussed by Yogananda in *Autobiography of a Yogi.* By attuning one's consciousness to this sound, one enters the stream of vibration that proceeded out of Spirit, and that emerges back into the Spirit at creation's end and at the end of the individual soul's cycle of outward wandering. By merging in AUM, liberation is attained.

OTHER TITLES IN THE MANTRA SERIES:
Gayatri Mantra ❀ *Mahamrityanjaya Mantra* ❀ *Maha Mantra*

BLISS CHANTS
Ananda Kirtan

Chanting focuses and lifts the mind to higher states of consciousness. *Bliss Chants* features chants written by Yogananda and his direct disciple, Swami Kriyananda. They're performed by Ananda Kirtan, a group of singers and musicians from Ananda, one of the world's most respected yoga communities. Chanting is accompanied by guitar, harmonium, kirtals, and tabla.

OTHER TITLES IN THE CHANT SERIES:
Divine Mother Chants ❀ *Power Chants* ❀ *Love Chants*
Peace Chants ❀ *Wisdom Chants* ❀ *Wellness Chants*

ANANDA SANGHA WORLDWIDE

Ananda Sangha is a fellowship of kindred souls following the teachings of Paramhansa Yogananda. The Sangha embraces the search for higher consciousness through the practice of meditation, and through the ideal of service to others in their quest for Self-realization. Approximately ten thousand spiritual seekers are affiliated with Ananda Sangha throughout the world.

Founded in 1968 by Swami Kriyananda, a direct disciple of Paramhansa Yogananda, Ananda includes seven communities in the United States, Europe, and in India. Worldwide, about one thousand devotees live in these spiritual communities, which are based on Yogananda's ideals of "plain living and high thinking."

Swami Kriyananda lived with his guru during the last four years of the Master's life, and continued to serve his organization for another ten years, bringing the teachings of Kriya Yoga and Self-realization to audiences in the United States, Europe, Australia, and, from 1958–1962, India. In 1968, together with a small group of close friends and students, he founded the first "world-brotherhood community" in the foothills of the Sierra Nevada Mountains in northeastern California. Initially a meditation retreat center located on sixty-seven acres of forested land, Ananda World-Brotherhood Community today encompasses one thousand acres where about 250 people live a dynamic, fulfilling life based on the principles and practices of spiritual, mental, and physical development, cooperation, respect, and divine friendship.

At this printing, after forty years of existence, Ananda is one of the most successful networks of intentional communities in the world. Urban communities have been developed in Palo Alto and Sacramento, California; Portland, Oregon; and Seattle, Washington. In Europe, near Assisi, Italy, a spiritual retreat and community was established in 1983, where today nearly one hundred residents from eight countries live. And in India, new communities have been founded in Gurgaon (near New Delhi) and in Pune.

THE EXPANDING LIGHT

We are visited by over two thousand people each year. Offering a varied, year-round schedule of classes and workshops on yoga, meditation, spiritual practices, yoga and meditation teacher training, and personal renewal retreats, The Expanding Light welcomes seekers from all backgrounds. Here you will find a loving, accepting environment, ideal for personal growth and spiritual renewal.

We strive to create an ideal relaxing and supportive environment for people to explore their own spiritual growth. We share the nonsectarian meditation practices and yoga philosophy of Paramhansa Yogananda and his direct disciple, Ananda's founder, Swami Kriyananda. Yogananda called his path "Self-realization," and our goal is to help our guests tune in to their own higher Selves.

Guests at The Expanding Light can learn the four practices that comprise Yogananda's teachings of Kriya Yoga: the Energization Exercises, the *Hong Sau* technique of concentration, the AUM technique, and Kriya Yoga. The first two techniques are available for all guests; the second two are available to those interested in pursuing this path more deeply.

Contact Information for Ananda Sangha Worldwide

mail: 14618 Tyler Foote Road • Nevada City, CA 95959
phone: 530.478.7560
online: www.ananda.org
email: sanghainfo@ananda.org

Contact Information the Expanding Light

mail: 14618 Tyler Foote Road • Nevada City, CA 95959
phone: 800.346.5350
online: www.expandinglight.org
email: info@expandinglight.org

CRYSTAL CLARITY PUBLISHERS

When you're seeking a book on practical spiritual living, you want to know it's based on an authentic tradition of timeless teachings, and that it resonates with integrity. This is the goal of Crystal Clarity Publishers: to offer you books of practical wisdom filled with true spiritual principles that have not only been tested through the ages, but also through personal experience.

We publish only books that combine creative thinking, universal principles, and a timeless message. Crystal Clarity books will open doors to help you discover more fulfillment and joy by living and acting from the center of peace within you.

Crystal Clarity Publishers—recognized worldwide for its bestselling, original, unaltered edition of Paramhansa Yogananda's classic *Autobiography of a Yogi*—offers many additional resources to assist you in your spiritual journey, including over one hundred books, a wide variety of inspirational and relaxation music composed by Swami Kriyananda (Yogananda's direct disciple), and yoga and meditation DVDs.

For our online catalog, complete with secure ordering, please visit us on the web at:

www.crystalclarity.com

Crystal Clarity music and audiobooks are available on all the popular online download sites. Look for us on your favorite online music website.

To request a catalog, place an order for the products you read about in the Further Explorations section of this book, or to find out more information about us and our products, please contact us:

Contact Information

mail:	14618 Tyler Foote Road
	Nevada City, CA 95959
phone:	800.424.1055 *or* 530.478.7600
online:	www.crystalclarity.com
email:	clarity@crystalclarity.com